Reaching Out Through Reading

Reaching Out Through Reading

Service Learning Adventures
with Literature

Carrie Sorby Duits

Adelle K. Dorman

Foreword by

Richard J. Kraft
Professor, University of Colorado—Boulder

1998
TEACHER IDEAS PRESS
A Division of
Libraries Unlimited, Inc.
Englewood, Colorado

This book is dedicated to all of the teachers who are willing to take a risk to demonstrate their caring for others by providing students the opportunity to learn through service.

We would like to sincerely thank our families, Tom, Jake, Nicole, Zach, and Barbara Duits and Curt Dorman, for their loving support.

TEACHER IDEAS PRESS
A Division of
Libraries Unlimited, Inc.
P.O. Box 6633
Englewood, CO 80155-6633
1-800-237-6124
www.lu.com/tip

Production Editor: Constance Hardesty
Proofreader: Lori Kranz
Layout: Pamela J. Getchell

Library of Congress Cataloging-in-Publication Data

Duits, Carrie Sorby, 1957-
  Reaching out through reading : service learning adventures with literature / Carrie Sorby Duits and Adelle K. Dorman ; foreword by Richard J. Kraft.
    x, 210 p. 22x28 cm.
    Includes index.
    ISBN 1-56308-514-3
    1. Student service.   2. Children's literature.   3. Children--Books and reading.   I. Dorman, Adelle K., 1970-   . II. Title.
LC220.5.D85 1998
372.64--dc21   98-11045
                                                              CIP

CONTENTS

Part 2—Children's Literature: Springboards to Service

Part 3—Service Learning Toolkit

LIST OF ILLUSTRATIONS

Worksheets

FOREWORD

    Service learning is a combination of words that has only recently entered the vocabulary of educational reformers, politicians, character educators and classroom practitioners, but in reality has a long and honorable history. While some of its manifestations can be found in the writings of John Dewey, it is a pedagogy with wide appeal across the ideological barriers. It traces some of its roots to volunteerism, but goes well beyond "doing good," and into the very curriculum of the school. While it seeks to build relationships to the community outside of the school, many of its most successful manifestations are in peer and cross-age tutoring programs within the building. While it can involve "picking up trash," and "working in the school office," it is much more appropriately related to teaching and learning academic concepts and skills. It is a way of connecting children and young people to the communities in a way that teaches civic responsibility and the roles of citizens in a democratic society. It is a pedagogy to make meaningful and relevant the lessons of almost any subject matter at any grade level. It is a mechanism for teaching character and values in an active, discovery manner. It is a way for teachers to delve more deeply into their disciplines or work between subjects in a multidisciplinary manner. Many reformers believe it to be the "Trojan horse of school reform," through the manner in which it changes the students, teachers, classrooms, schools and communities in which it is best practiced.

    In *Reaching Out Through Reading,* Carrie Duits and Adelle Dorman provide classroom teachers with not only a solid introduction to the meaning of service learning, but also a practical list of ways to get started. The service learning field is filled with general books on ways teachers can tie their classrooms to the broader community, and there are numerous books on "how to teach literature," but there is a dearth of books that tell the teacher how to do service learning in a specific subject area, such as children's literature. This book breaks new ground in providing the teacher with detailed ways in which the study of children's literature can be a springboard for service learning. The authors have provided detailed summaries of 20 children's books, in which they have found the seeds of service. Busy teachers will find important messages to gain from each book, along with suggested service projects, related literature, discussion questions and vocabulary, reflections, and finally activity sheets. In other words, while conceptually sound, this book will give the teacher an excellent handle on how to not only begin service learning activities with children, but ties it beautifully into the ongoing reading and writing program of any school.

If service learning is ever to live up to its potential, it must be woven into the day-to-day lives of teachers and students and more deeply into the regular curriculum of the school. One can only hope that other teachers will take up the challenge to do in the other curricular areas what Duits and Dorman have done so beautifully in children's literature.

Richard J. Kraft
Professor, University of Colorado—Boulder
Author and editor, *Building Community: Service Learning in the Academic Disciplines*

Part 1

Introduction to Service Learning

Why Service Learning?

How to Service Learn

WHY SERVICE LEARNING?

While we were sharing service learning activities with a class of fourth graders, an innocent-looking student looked up and declared, "I can't think of anyone who needs help." We were sad and angry that this student wasn't aware of the needs of his immediate community. We were fearful that this comment reflected a growing societal dilemma. But is our world any different today than it was in the past?

Our society has evolved in such a way that our youth encounter hurdles that previous generations did not. With an increased absence of adult role models, there are widening gaps in social development (Hahn and Danzberger 1987). Many children are missing the guidance they need from adults. Passive recreation in front of the television bombards them with violence. Responsibilities and expectations have gone from working the fields to running the dishwasher. Who is responsible for teaching our young to be productive, empathetic, caring individuals? Our fast-paced society is not going to slow down enough to answer this question. As teachers, it is our responsibility to extend our classroom's learning environment into areas that will nurture compassion, community participation, and civic education. Although these ideas are not always embraced by the formal curriculum, Kraft (1986) encourages, "Don't give up hope. Although educational change and reform is slow, all good ideas began small and then spread from class to class, school to school, state to state and eventually nation to nation" (p. 2).

SERVICE LEARNING: A CASE FOR CIVIC EDUCATION

Public education is the one right given to all children in America. It is a right that carries increasing responsibilities with our changing society. According to Nel Noddings (1992), we should educate our children to be not only competent individuals, but also people who are caring, loving, and lovable. Schools are already taking enormous responsibility in the partnership of raising children to be knowledgeable, caring citizens. Today's schools teach life skills, such as drug awareness, conflict management, sex education, and multicultural appreciation. In addition, schools also provide counseling, before- and after-school care, subsidized lunches, and a variety of other services. John Silber (1989) writes, "[T]he school cannot achieve its academic goals without providing caring and continuity for students."

Realizing a need for children to learn care and compassion, schools are attempting to integrate theory by designing programs, sometimes with misguided and incomplete information. Schools are attempting to save children, children at risk in a nation at risk (Fine 1991). One theory that addresses the issue of learning to care is *service learning*. Service learning can be a powerful vehicle for teaching students to care.

WHAT IS SERVICE LEARNING?

Service learning is a theory born out of the philosophy of active, integrative education. It is a call for students and teachers to assume responsibility within their community through experience-based learning. Meaningful service learning must combine experience with academic development. Through these opportunities, students reach out to others, promoting the development of empathy. When this is an ongoing process, students may develop a greater sensitivity for others. An ethic of care leads to designing service learning projects that speak to the needs of the community, ultimately fulfilling the students' need to give. Service learning

combines academics with community service.

strives to benefit the served and the server.

promotes an ethic of care, resulting in increased empathy for the server.

promotes student leadership through project ownership.

sets the stage for learning civic responsibility.

Service Learning: Common Misconceptions

One misconception of service learning surfaced when one of the author's sons registered for his classes in middle school. He chose service learning as one of his two electives. Proudly, she signed the registration, believing that her own dedication to service had inspired him. Her dreams were shattered when she discovered that "Service Learning"—as defined by his school—meant that he would be an office aide for one period each day. The school had simply taken the ideas of service and citizenship and tailored them to fit its needs. Parents, students, and teachers alike are forming this deficient and erroneous definition of service learning. Service learning *must* combine academics with community service.

Another gross misconception of service learning was revealed at a district meeting to discuss the new requirements of middle school students. A committee presented the requirements with a note at the bottom of the proposal that stated, "The committee values service learning, but feels it needs to be coordinated to provide a meaningful, sequential experience for students." When asked for clarification, the response was that budget cuts would not allow for service learning to continue. There would be no money to hire a coordinator. The implications of this decision are numerous. First, it implies that schools cannot participate in service learning without budgeting a large sum of money for it. This district also believes that service learning requires a coordinator to facilitate the program. Service learning becomes an add-on feature to a student's school day. All these assumptions lead to a superficial level of commitment to service learning as well as a misconception of a program that is vital in the development of our youth. This book allows teachers to provide their students with service learning opportunities without costly coordinators.

Service learning is becoming more and more prevalent in the classroom (Simons 1994). Many schools attempt to integrate service into their regular curricula. Unfortunately, when service learning is introduced to an educational community, it is frequently a concept that is only partially understood. Although many schools are requiring or offering service classes, it is often not being integrated into the regular curriculum, and therefore the learning portion of "service learning" is lacking. In this way, service can be "miseducative" (Dewey 1938), giving children the misconception that volunteerism is synonymous with service learning.

Myths About Service Learning

One of the most difficult aspects of developing service learning projects is knowing how to make them operative within existing constraints. Project developers must move from conceptualizing theories of ideal programs to designing a program that is both ideal and practical. Misconceptions regarding the implementation of service learning lead to perceived obstacles. These obstacles are merely myths.

Myth 1: Teachers must have a primary leadership role in service learning projects.

Reality: The planning and implementation stages must be participant/youth centered. This gives students ownership of the project, thereby making it more meaningful for the learners. When ideas are introduced by the teacher, the students need to have the opportunity to select, modify or expand the initial proposals.

Student ownership in service learning begins by arousing interest. At first, incorporating areas of student interest with community needs will provide the needed incentive. Later, growth in the areas of caring, empathy, and community may become a sufficient catalyst to service. Therefore, when starting out, it is important to allow students to have ownership in order to best nurture their growth.

Myth 2: Service does not have to incorporate an academic component in order to be "service learning."

Reality: Service learning must be integrated in a significant way in the academic curriculum.

Myth 3: Support from the principal is not necessary.

Reality: There must be a commitment of support from the school. Regardless of what form this support takes, it is necessary in case any problems arise.

Myth 4: Resources are not available for service learning.

Reality: Meaningful and necessary service must be provided for the community. One of the biggest obstacles in the acceptance and practice of service learning on a widespread basis is the lack of resources available in the classroom. Although there are limited prepared materials available to the elementary teacher, the ability to care is the only true foundational resource required. This book provides practical examples of how to implement meaningful service learning projects with a limited budget—or no budget at all.

Myth 5: The needs of the served are more important than the needs of the server.

Reality: The service must address special needs, developmental levels, and concerns of the served. These issues are just as relevant for the servers. The server is an essential part of the service learning formula, and both parties should benefit.

In service learning, depth is always more important than breadth. Therefore, implementation should always occur without sacrificing meaning in order to meet artificially constructed classroom objectives. Students should not be constrained by rigid classroom-established objectives of service. For example, a student who is reading to a nursing home patient may find that the patient prefers to visit. The student should not be confined to the established objective of reading to patients.

Myth 6: Service learning lessens students' academic development.

Reality: Service learning *is* academic development. In order to insure academic growth, students must be given an opportunity to reflect on their service and relate it to classroom curriculum. This step is one that is often overlooked, because of time constraints. It is an essential element of any true service learning project. From our experiences, the small number of teachers who know about service learning perceive it as something extracurricular to be added if there is extra time. In these cases, service learning is not understood as a method that can be used to greatly enhance the regular curriculum. When used appropriately, service learning can add depth of understanding to any school subject (Simons 1994). Ralph Tyler (1949) contends that experience should help to fulfill the needs and interests of the learner. Properly conducted, service learning projects do just that. They spring forth from the interests of the class, satisfying the needs of the giver (especially in the areas of social and academic growth) as well as those of the receiver.

Service Learning: The Apple of the Community's Eye

The six myths just debunked highlight the components essential to any service learning project. Each of these components must be in place in order for service learning to be successfully implemented. Although we recognize that it is challenging to incorporate all of the components, each is a necessary piece of a true service learning experience. Together, these six components may be examined metaphorically as an apple tree.

1. The planning and implementation stages must be participant/youth centered and student designed. This component may be visualized as the roots of the tree. Just as each root contributes to the whole, each student makes important contributions to the service learning project.

2. Service learning must be integrated in a significant way into the academic curriculum, providing hands-on experience for the material. Using the apple tree metaphor, this component may be seen as the trunk. Springing from the roots (the participants), the curriculum provides support for the rest of the tree. Service learning must be supported by this base of classroom learning.

3. There must be a commitment of support from the school principal. As the branches of the tree must be strong, so must this support. Weak branches endanger the service learning project.

4. Meaningful and necessary service must be provided for the served community. Like the leaves on an apple tree, making the service meaningful and necessary provides an important blanket over the project. This blanket of service is not only important for those served, but it aids in validating the experience in the minds of the servers. Like leaves, this validating component supplies energy to service learning projects.

5. The service must address special needs, developmental levels, and concerns of both the server and the served. The tree's fruits, or service projects, are unique to individual situations and community needs. Service satisfies the needs of the community, much as an apple satisfies the needs of the hungry.

6. The students must be given an opportunity to reflect on their service and relate it to classroom curriculum. This final component may be compared to the shadow of the apple tree. Reflecting on the experience connects the project to the classroom at the roots, or the participants. The shadow of the tree is always there, even as the tree changes and grows.

Supporting the Leap from Theory to Practice

Service learning nurtures personal development. It involves an ethic of care, a sense of community, and gaining empathy for others. Service learning strengthens students' emotional intelligence while making connections for students between academics and the real world. Through authentic experiences and interactions with their community, students gain an understanding of the responsibilities of citizenship in a democracy.

A main goal of service learning is to promote the development of empathetic and sensitive citizens. Nel Noddings (1992) is a strong proponent of an "ethic of care" as a function of education. She abolishes the notion of academic learning taking precedence over the social development of children: "Those who care must attend to the other, must feel that surge of energy flowing toward the other's needs and projects. Caring is a capacity (or set of capacities) that requires cultivation. It requires time." Noddings invites educators to encourage students to reach out to people in their community. Service learning makes this possible.

Sergiovanni: Building Community

Thomas Sergiovanni believes that the heart of teaching is a commitment to the ethic of caring. The result is more powerful student learning rather than a compromise of academic standards. In *Building Community in Schools* (1994), Sergiovanni proclaims the need for building a sense of belonging. Being connected to others, to ideas, and to values adds meaning to students' lives. Service learning projects give students a worthy cause that nurtures a sense of belonging.

How can students demonstrate an ethic of care? One way is through service learning. Academics are not sacrificed, and students benefit from meaningful learning experiences that enrich the curriculum. The community of learners becomes a community with purpose through service learning.

Covey: Empathy

Stephen Covey, in his book *The Seven Habits of Highly Effective People* (1989), lists empathy as one of the seven qualities of successful and effective people. Through empathetic listening, we seek first to understand others' feelings. To communicate effectively with others, we must understand their perceptions. The result is an appreciation of differences. Empathy demonstrates our sensitivity to others. Students who develop empathy for others also develop concern and sincerity. A goal of this book is for students to become sensitive, caring members of their community. Service learning helps students build character and develop as effective individuals.

Developing our ability to care fosters empathy. Empathy is knowing how to interpret others' emotions. It involves reading and responding to spoken and unspoken feelings. One goal of teaching students to be empathetic is for them to see human problems and to want to become part of the solution. This creates a strong connection between the academic curriculum and service learning. Students experience real-life dilemmas from the stories of others' lives.

Goleman: Emotional Intelligence

In his book *Emotional Intelligence*, Daniel Goleman (1995) synthesizes the science of current brain research to assert that there is more to intelligence than using our cognitive ability. Goleman purports that our emotional intelligence, or EQ, is a greater indicator of success in life than our IQ. This makes it critical for educators to incorporate the emotional development of students by integrating the process into the curriculum.

The root of all the components of emotional intelligence is the ability to empathize with others (Goleman 1995). Integrating lessons of empathy through literature will help students develop their EQ. Service learning allows students to demonstrate and develop their emotional intelligence.

Caine and Caine: Making Connections

Caine and Caine (1991) suggest that learning is a complex process. Their research supports "talking, listening, reading, viewing, acting, and valuing" (p. 6) through the use of many types of learning theories. Incorporating service learning into the academic curriculum provides opportunities to maximize connections between content and experience. These experiences provide meaning by integrating learning with real-life situations. By combining service experiences with learning, students make connections to real-life events. This book provides one avenue for students to explore real-life situations by introducing them to characters and situations in quality children's literature.

John Dewey: Experience-Based Education

According to John Dewey (1938), experience-based education programs are essential. Quality of experience must be emphasized in order to achieve depth in learning. Dewey's ideal learning environment stresses community work, responsibility, and a strong group contribution. This provides internal social control within the classroom. For example, it has been shown that the behavior of at-risk students often improves when they are participating in a service learning project they consider to be of intrinsic value (Calbrese and Schumer 1986).

Becoming learned citizens who can participate knowledgeably in a democracy is the most fundamental issue of education for Dewey (1938), Tyler (1949), and Barbar (1992). Each believes that schooling needs to be based on democratic values. They all contend that there is a necessary link between school and society, a link that is practically invisible on the most fundamental level—that of the student. In addition, each believes that children enter the classroom without a foundation of liberty; that liberty is not natural, but taught. Liberty must be integrated with a call to service. By introducing community service as a valuable component of the learning process, it is hoped that service will become a habit in each individual's life.

THE MANY WAYS SERVICE LEARNING AFFECTS STUDENTS

Preventing Dropout

Service learning is a viable curriculum alternative for the at-risk population. Research has shown that many at-risk students are self-motivated and are fully capable of mastering the academics they encounter in school (Reyes 1989). However, this is a population that has, for the most part, tuned out or been tuned out to regular classroom learning. Service learning provides a more individualized approach that is complemented by student ownership and enriched life experiences. These qualities may make school more intrinsically valuable to the at-risk student. Allowing students to reach for meaningful and relevant goals within their community provides a bridge for learning experiences inside and outside of the classroom (Simons 1994). As Wells (1990) states, "Early intervention is recognized as crucial to limiting the perpetuation of students at risk in later years" (p. 11). This indicates that service learning can be especially helpful for dropout prevention.

Promoting Leadership

By providing safe opportunities to realize their civic calling, students may be more apt to assume leadership positions within their community and within their classrooms. The development of a sense of empathy and caring, civic duty, and experience with needs in the community has the potential to nurture leadership in students. Gandhi claimed that leadership arises out of service. In his opinion, only by providing service based in truth and nonviolence will others be inclined to truly follow. This is a leadership founded on ideas of giving rather than gain. It is a leadership earned and not demanded. It is a leadership based on compassion and care.

Appreciating Diversity

Service learning is one gateway to multicultural education. By serving in various sectors of their community, students may become acquainted with root social issues, such as race, gender, ethnicity, socio-economics, and sexual orientation. Exposure to such issues can help to foster understanding of others and make for a more tolerant community.

Encouraging Active Citizenship

Service learning shows students the importance of civic participation. Following are quotes from fifth-grade students who have been involved in service learning. A strong link between participation and citizenship can be seen.

Question: What does it take to be a good citizen?

Good citizens help people. If someone is lost, then they'll give them directions. If someone is hurt, even if they're not too good at healing, they'll try to help. I think it's mostly just trying, trying your best.

To serve the community . . . to help with the community, like the homeless . . . and all of the people that don't have anything to eat, or donating money or food for the homeless.

Being able to help other people, and if someone was hurt, you would help them or call for help, that would be a good citizen, but if you didn't help, if you were like, 'nah, I'm not going to help,' then that wouldn't be good citizenship.

To help out when you can. Like in [our] community, you can't help all of the time, but the little things that you can help do, then that helps to make everyone a leader, if they help to do the little things.

Developing Conflict Management Skills

Service learning allows students to use and strengthen their conflict-management skills. By working together in common ownership of a service project, students assume certain roles and must be accountable for them. Roles or ideas may be challenged as the classroom community learns to work together in a service learning environment.

INTEGRATING SERVICE LEARNING INTO THE CURRICULUM

Several schools offer something they call service learning, but it is confined to school filing or hall monitoring. This is not service learning. Service learning must always include an aspect of learning that is connected to the classroom curriculum. Often, the six main components of service learning are ignored in these situations. This makes the service a type of mandatory volunteerism, but in no way qualifies the service as service learning. Service learning may include service to the school, but it must be a service adjoined with classroom learning. The continuum of service may also extend to individuals or to large communities. The service experience may be in a student's backyard or across the world. The breadth of service is not important, rather, it is the depth that adds meaning to the service component of service learning.

REFERENCES

Barbar, B. 1992. *An Aristocracy of Everyone: The Politics of Education and the Future of America.* New York: Oxford University Press.

Brooks, J., and M. Brooks. 1993. *In Search of Understanding: The Case for Constructivist Classrooms.* Alexandria, VA: Association for Supervision and Curriculum Development.

Caine, R. N., and G. Caine. 1991. *Making Connections: Teaching and the Human Brain.* Menlo Park, CA: Addison-Wesley Publishing Company.

Calbrese, R. L., and H. Schumer. 1986. "The Effects of Service Activities on Adolescent Alienation." *Adolescents* 21: 665–87.

Covey, S. R. 1989. *The Seven Habits of Highly Effective People: Restoring the Character Ethic.* New York: Simon and Schuster.

Dewey, J. 1938. *Experience and Education.* New York: Macmillan.

Evans, R. J. 1984. "Fostering Peer Acceptance of Handicapped Students." *ERIC Digest* 1406: 1.

Fine, Michelle. 1991. *Framing Dropouts.* Albany: State University of New York Press.

Goleman, D. 1995. *Emotional Intelligence.* New York: Bantam Books.

Hahn, A., and J. Danzberger. March 1987. *Dropouts in America: Enough Is Known for Action.* Washington, DC: Institute for Educational Leadership Publications Department.

Kraft, R. 1986. "Editorial: 1984: The Orwellian Year of Educational Politics and Reform." In *Experiential Education and the Schools,* edited by R. Kraft and J. Kielsmeir, 2d ed. Boulder, CO: Association for Experiential Education.

Noddings, N. 1992. *The Challenge to Care in Schools: An Alternative Approach to Education.* New York: Teacher's College Press.

Reyes, P. 1989. "Factors That Affect the Commitment of Children at Risk to Stay in School." In *Children at Risk,* ed. by J. M. Lakebrink. Chicago: Charles C. Thomas Publications.

Sergiovanni, T. J. 1994. *Building Community in Schools.* San Francisco: Jossey-Bass.

Silber, John. 1989. *Straight Shooting: What's Wrong with America and How to Fix It.* New York: Harper & Row.

Simons, P. 1994. "A Call to Service: Merging the Hearts and Minds of America's Young Children: Elementary School Service Learning." In *Building Community: Service Learning in the Academic Disciplines,* ed. by R. J. Kraft and M. Swadener. Denver: Colorado Campus Compact.

Tyler, R. 1949. *Basic Principals of Curriculum and Instruction.* Chicago: University of Chicago Press.

Wells, S. E. 1990. *At-Risk Youth: Identification, Programs, and Recommendations.* Englewood, CO: Teacher Ideas Press.

HOW TO SERVICE LEARN

GETTING STARTED: READ-ALOUD TIME

Read-aloud time is a wonderful opportunity to begin the discussion that gives birth to service learning projects. Most elementary teachers find time each day or week to read aloud to students or to share a favorite book. Reading aloud to students has multiple benefits. It is an opportunity for teachers to share their enthusiasm for reading. This enthusiasm brings students together as they share a common story. Reading aloud improves listening skills and aids reading comprehension (Routman 1991). It promotes literature appreciation as well as an understanding of the author's message and the writing process (Cooper 1993). Reading aloud also encourages listening carefully and understanding others and their situations—two skills that are critical in the development of empathy. Thus, through read-alouds, students discover the characters' needs while involved in academic growth.

According to J. David Cooper (1993), there are seven guidelines for planning read-aloud time in the classroom:

- ❖ Select a consistent time and read aloud every day.
- ❖ Provide a comfortable, inviting place in the classroom for reading aloud.
- ❖ Select high-quality books that both you and the students will enjoy.
- ❖ Read with expression and emotion.
- ❖ Allow time for discussion during and after the read-aloud time period.
- ❖ Do not use the discussion time to test students.
- ❖ Permit students to write or draw during the reading.

Each of these guidelines supports the development of service learning projects. The most critical, however, is reading with expression and emotion. The teacher's attitude and enthusiasm contribute greatly to the success of the project. Reading the book with feeling and sensitivity will motivate students to want to develop meaningful service learning projects.

Using This Book

Service learning can easily be integrated into a literature-based reading program. The units described in this book are designed to be adapted to a variety of teaching methods. Each unit has a main literature choice, activities to bridge the literature to service learning projects, related literature suggestions for independent reading or enrichment, discussion questions, vocabulary lists, and possible service projects.

Adapting the Literature Units to Fit Your Reading Program

Either the main literature choice or the related literature should be used for read aloud to provide ample opportunity for discussion about the characters, their situation, and the meaning that the reading has to individuals in the class. Each teacher needs to select an appropriate plan, depending on the reading program in place in the classroom. Some of the possibilities are as follows:

- ❖ Students read related literature for independent reading or individual or small group instruction, and the teacher reads the main literature choice as a read-aloud book.

- ❖ Students read the main literature choice, and the teacher shares related literature during read-aloud time.

- ❖ Students read related literature to book buddies, and the teacher reads the main selection as a read-aloud book.

Book Summaries and Important Messages

Book summaries have been included for the teacher's convenience. These summaries outline the important messages of each book and can act as a reference for teachers seeking certain types of service learning projects. The summaries highlight some of the most essential and affective components of the literature.

Activity Bridge to Service Learning

For each book there is an activity that helps students connect the ideas in the literature to the development of a service learning project. The activity bridge helps students take a closer look at the deeper meaning of the story. Each activity bridge includes a worksheet for students to use in organizing their thoughts and begin the work of designing service projects.

Related Literature

A section devoted to related literature is included for each selected book. This section has been included to help the classroom teacher extend the main ideas of the primary book. The related literature provides students with a broader scope than can be provided by a single book. These supplements can be used during sustained silent reading. Another way that the related literature can be incorporated into the classroom is through small group exploration. Here, character and situational descriptions can provide a link between texts and service issues. Related literature can also provide students of varying reading abilities an opportunity to explore themes at levels more or less challenging than the selected book.

Suggested Service Learning Projects

Incorporating a service learning project may seem intimidating at first. The suggested examples are provided to make the teacher and students aware of some of the possibilities for service. Keep in mind the service learning projects suggested for each book are simply examples. Students should have an opportunity to share their own suggestions or to modify the given examples. The suggested possibilities for service extend from the server being completely removed from the served, as in the case of fund-raising, to direct involvement with the served community, as in the case of visiting a nursing home. Regardless of the degree of involvement with the served community, all suggested service learning projects provide deep possibilities for growth.

Discussion Questions

Discussions that are focused on the books' characters and their needs help students relate to the characters. The discussions allow students to discover the author's message by thoughtfully considering the characters' situations. Students may ask themselves what they would do if they were in a similar situation, or how they would feel. These are common questions for each reading because they allow the students to interact with the story. In addition, allowing students to make predictions and inferences during the read-aloud sessions helps them think critically about the problems presented in the literature. These critical-thinking skills lead to the development of meaningful service learning projects.

The teacher's attitude and enthusiasm during discussions are an important aspect in the development of meaningful service learning projects. The teacher must provide adequate background information during prereading discussions to motivate students to explore the literature with an intent to develop service learning projects. Discussion gives students an opportunity to express their opinions and to begin to own the project that results from the reading. Focused discussions can contribute to meaningful, participant-centered projects.

One option for conducting discussion groups is to draw upon the ideas of the Socratic Seminar. These seminars are based on student-centered discussions. Ideally, a student leader plays the role of facilitator, asking questions that are related to a text. The purposes of these questions are to bring out multiple perspectives, gain a more clear and deeper understanding of the text, and encourage students to justify their thinking by referencing the text. Participation in Socratic Seminars may be used as a part of the assessment within a service learning unit. The ground rules of a Socratic Seminar are:

❖ Come prepared to discuss the topic.

❖ Pass when you have nothing to contribute.

❖ Ask for clarification of confusing issues.

❖ Use the text to reference your ideas. Stay away from opinions unless you clarify them as such.

❖ Stay on task and focus on the issue.

❖ Take turns speaking. Socratic Seminars don't require hand raising.

❖ Listen respectfully to everyone's opinion.

❖ Talk to each other, not to the facilitator. (Gray n.d.)

Socratic Seminars force students to think about their own opinions, and to consider alternate points of view. It should be remembered that the purpose of these seminars is to provide students the opportunity to express themselves in a generally atypical forum. Although the teacher may feel that he or she has important information to share, the Socratic Seminar is generally not the place to do it. The teacher's role, if any, should be to provide redirection and coaching. When first conducting the Socratic Seminar, teachers may worry when there is a lull in the discussion. However, this "dead time" should be accepted as a part of the seminar. Encourage students to use the lulls to think about issues in the text. Socratic Seminars are an excellent way to create a foundation of main ideas in the text. Understanding these ideas can lead students to brainstorming service learning projects.

Journals and Reading Logs

Students may also respond to the discussion questions in writing. Journals and reading logs offer students the opportunity to express their thoughts and concerns about issues raised in the reading. The questions are designed to help students reflect and to share similar experiences and prior knowledge. Through reflective journal responses and follow-up discussions that focus on the characters' situation and emotions, students see things in new ways. Students interact with the literature in an empathetic way, which can lead naturally to service learning.

Another type of journal response is the two-way journal. One way of writing a two-way journal is to have the students divide their papers into two columns. In the first column, they write about a situation from the book. In the second column, they write about a similar situation of concern in their community. Another way to approach two-way journaling is to write a direct quote from the text in the first column and have the student respond in the second column. Students can share their written journal responses as a part of the group brainstorming session in which various service options are proposed.

Vocabulary

The vocabulary lists provided for each literature unit can be used in a variety of ways. Because true service learning incorporates an academic aspect, vocabulary words should be used to build understanding of the book's meaning. The vocabulary activities should not overshadow the main goal of reading the book, which is to develop empathy for and understanding of the characters and their unique situations.

Setting Up a Service Learning Project

The selected texts shuttle students into worlds that may or may not be familiar to them. Through discussion and reflection, students are encouraged to grow as individuals within their community. Using their acquired awareness to reach out to the community, students can acquire a new sense of the meaning of service. The project examples provide a connection between the selected literature and the real needs of the community.

Many logistical issues must be addressed when setting up a service learning project. Students should assume responsibility for as much of the project as possible, such as initiating and following up on phone conversations with service recipients.

To begin, the class must be sure that it can actually provide the service students wish to offer. Students must also understand the reasons they are doing the service learning project. Ideally, the reasons should be generated from the students. Encourage students to establish some expectations for the project. Have them reflect on their reasons for serving. Ask them to evaluate whether their expectations were met after the project is complete. Often, it is also helpful for students to do some on-site reflection of the reasons why they are serving, if time allows.

(Text continues on p. 24.)

BRAINSTORMING

Brainstorming helps a group create a list of many possible project ideas in an organized fashion. This technique allows students to see all the dimensions of a service learning project. In structured brainstorming, each person in the group offers an idea in turn. It requires all students to contribute. Unstructured brainstorming, on the other hand, allows students to share ideas as they come to mind. Regardless of the method used to create a list of ideas for service learning projects, there are certain brainstorming guidelines to follow. *The Memory Jogger for Education* (GOAL/QPC 1992) suggests the following guidelines:

- Everyone should have a firm understanding of the issue being brainstormed.
- Never question or criticize the ideas of students.
- Write every student idea on the chart.
- Record the idea in the students' exact words.
- Work quickly.

Many tools can help students brainstorm. The tools can be made of butcher paper, written on the chalkboard, or copied onto a transparency.

We have selected Jane Cowen-Fletcher's *It Takes a Village* to illustrate how various brainstorming tools can be used to generate a list of service learning projects. The important messages in the book can be used to identify service learning projects that address the needs of the class or the community. *It Takes a Village* has several important messages, including:

- There is joy in helping others.
- Everyone contributes something important to the group.
- We need to be responsible for our actions.
- It is good to ask for help when we need it.
- Expressing gratitude is important.
- The village is a place where people look out for each other.

After reading the book to students, discuss the messages as a springboard for brainstorming service learning projects. The following brainstorming tools are designed to facilitate the development of a meaningful, participant-centered service learning project. Blank masters for these tools can be found in part 3.

Three-Column Brainstorming

One method of allowing students to incorporate their interests into service learning is three-column brainstorming (see fig. 2.1). In the first column, students list their interests (for example, soccer, reading, drama). In the second column, students list important messages in the book (for example, being thankful, accepting responsibility, looking after each other). Viewing these lists side by side, students create a third list, combining their interests with needs found in the book in order to find a way to serve. Students should make these lists individually, before group brainstorming.

Your Interests	Important Messages from the Book	Service Possibilities
Writing	There is joy in helping others.	Start a school market to sell school supplies and items.
Football	Everyone contributes something to the group.	Establish class buddies with students in a younger or older class.
Movies	We need to be responsible for our actions.	Begin a babysitting club.
Cooking	It is good to ask for help when we need it.	Have a food or clothing drive.
Playing piano	Expressing gratitude is important.	Write thank-you letters to the people who have helped you.

Fig. 2.1. Three-column brainstorming helps students match their interests to existing needs.

The Web to Service

A web allows students to piggyback ideas as they are developed. Webs may be used to visually stimulate topics for discussion. Webs link ideas to a primary theme or focus. A web may be easily constructed by placing the title of the book in the center of the web. Students then brainstorm the important messages found in the book. The final step is brainstorming project ideas that address these concerns or issues. Although the example in figure 2.2 includes only one action per issue, students will be able to brainstorm many more.

Three-Way Journal Response

This tool expands the two-way journal response (discussed on page 19). During the brainstorming session, students add a third column to their two-way journal response. In the third column they list possible service learning projects based on their responses in the second column of their journal entry. (See fig. 2.3.) After students have had an opportunity to explore project possibilities, students may share their written journal responses during a group brainstorming session.

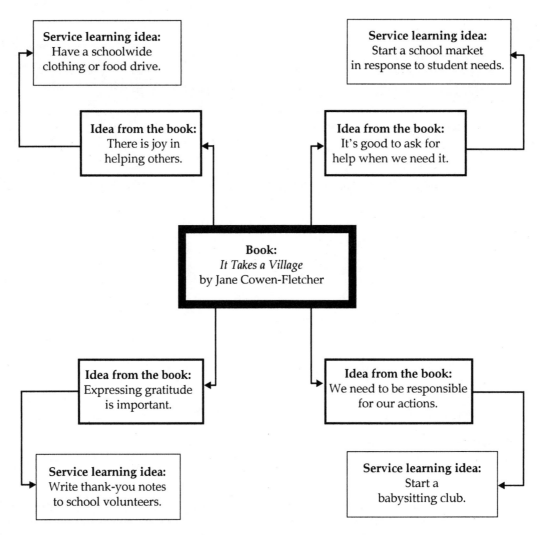

Fig. 2.2. The web to service structure leads students from a book's main messages to service learning projects.

Issue or Quote from the Book	Community Issue or Response to Quote	Possible Service Learning Project
It takes a village.	At school, many people help me throughout the day.	Write thank-you letters to school personnel and volunteers.

Fig. 2.3. The three-way journal response encourages students to brainstorm ideas for service learning projects based on their previous journal writing.

Reflective Windows

Present students with a metaphor of a house with many floors, or stories. Explain that the messages in every book lend themselves to many situations. On butcher paper, draw a house with many floors, or levels, and several windows on each floor. Explain that the house as a whole represents the book *It Takes a Village,* and each level, or floor, of the house represents a different community need, such as hunger, thirst, and shelter. Display the drawing in the classroom during the unit. Ask students to reflect on one of the community needs and propose a service project to address that need. Students write their suggestions on squares of paper. Students then place their squares on the appropriate part of the house. (The squares on which students' suggestions are written create the "reflective windows" of the house. See fig. 2.4.)

Blank forms for each of these brainstorming tools can be found in part 3.

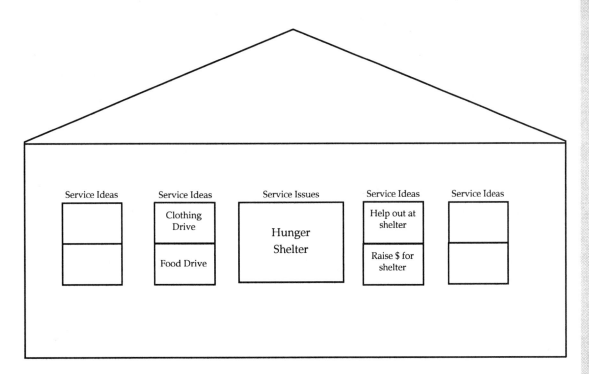

Fig. 2.4. Reflective windows allow students to see how many related ideas come together.

BRAINSTORMING BRAINSTORMING

The Project Discussion Frame (see fig. 2.5) helps to lend meaning to the beginning stages of the service learning project. It requires students to consider the reasons why they should or should not invest themselves in such a project. What will the students gain? What will the served gain?

One method for selecting the most viable service learning project is to work through a series of worksheets (provided in part 3). Begin the process using the From Character Needs to Community Needs reproducible to generate ideas for who needs help in your community. Afterwards, the entire class can brainstorm service learning projects using the various brainstorming tools. Then, students may propose their projects to the whole group on the Project Discussion Frame reproducible. Students may work on the worksheet in small groups, with each group analyzing the pros and cons of one proposed project. (All reproducibles appear in part 3.)

Next, decide how the class will select a specific service learning project. Students may express their interests and community commitment individually or in small groups. Or, using a democratic system, the whole class may vote to select one service learning project in which everyone participates. Each of these options comes with benefits as well as problems. If there is not a pre-established classroom method for reaching consensus, consider having the class examine the pros and cons of each idea before selecting the most viable option. After sufficient discussion (using the Project Discussion Frame reproducible in part 3, for example) students may vote on a service project. (One way to vote is dot voting. Each student is given three dots and may distribute the dots among the various choices.) The method used to select a service learning project will vary, depending on the needs of the class, the needs of the community, and the facilitator's comfort level.

After the class has selected a service learning project, the Project Planner reproducible (in part 3) may be used to explore the academic components of the project. The planner also helps students with the initial steps of the project, such as seeking permission and identifying required resources.

At this point in the process, the project may be further organized by using the Project Details or Project Timeline reproducibles (both in part 3). Several model letters, a form requesting support, and a phone script also appear in part 3.

Finally, as the project evolves from the development process into the actual service learning project, the teacher must monitor to be sure the project follows all the guidelines for service learning:

student centered and student designed

academic aspects

support from the school

meaningful and necessary focus

addressing individual needs

reflection

Project Discussion Frame

Patients might
not have family
who write.

It will give us
practice writing.

It will help me
better understand
the elderly.

**Reasons To
Do the Project**

Service Learning Project Idea

Write letters to patients
in local nursing home.

**Reasons Not To
Do the Project**

Patients might be
too old to read.

They might not
write back.

I don't understand
old people.

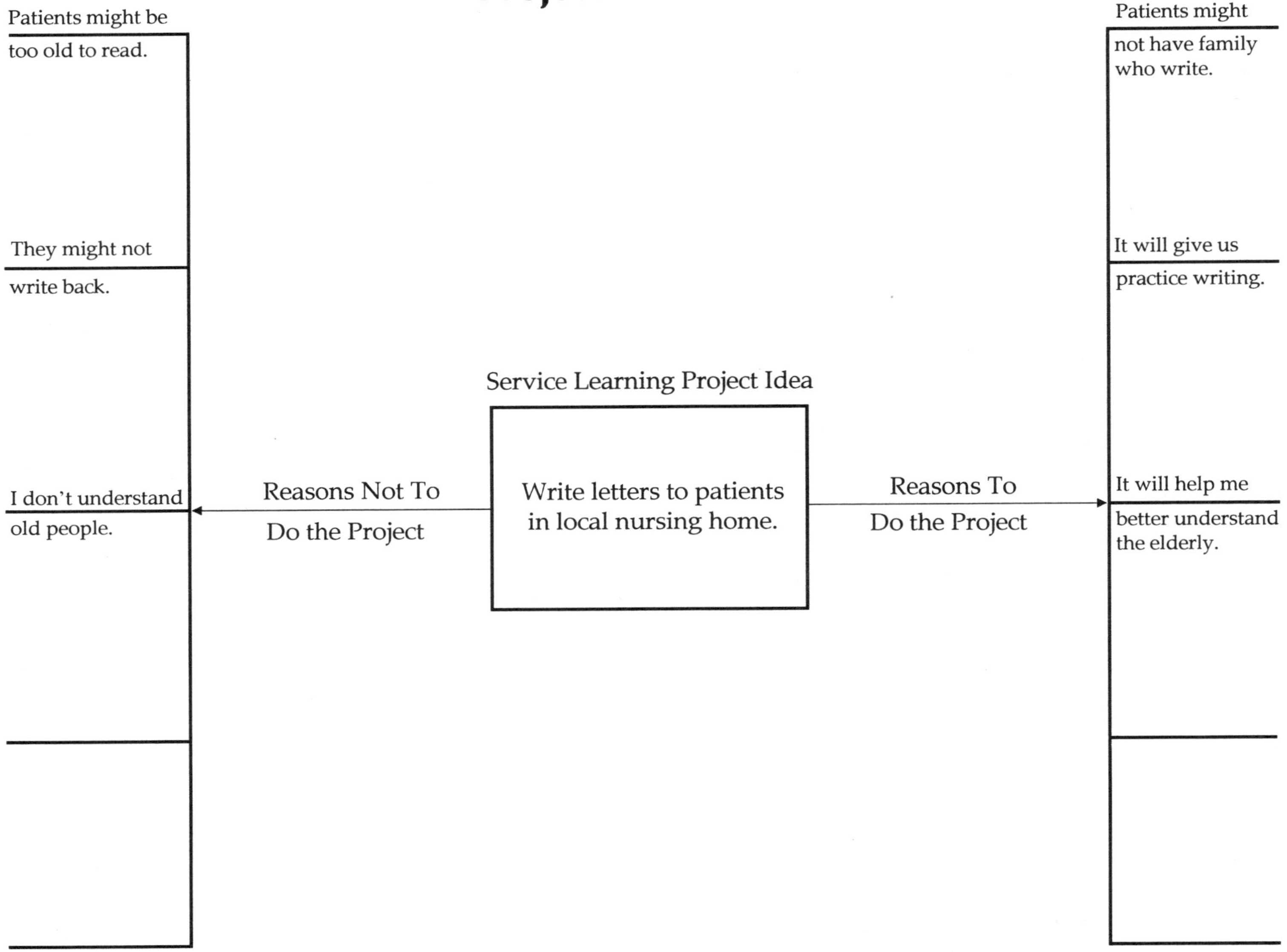

Fig. 2.5. The Project Discussion Frame helps students weigh the benefits and costs involved in the service learning project.

Service Learning Project Considerations

Several key issues must be addressed when planning a service learning project. Planning will help to ensure the project's success. Some of the most important issues are:

Time. The recipient of your service must understand how much time you can commit to the project. This is important not only out of consideration for the recipient, but because it may influence the type of service that you do. Don't forget to figure in transportation time and the time it will take for students to get organized.

Safety. Student safety must never be compromised. The concept of student safety applies to all aspects: physical, emotional, spiritual, and moral. Individual beliefs should never be violated in the name of building community awareness or heightening civic understanding.

Supervision. Adult–child ratios for field trips will have to be taken into consideration, and volunteers recruited as necessary. If your school is near a university, the teacher education program may be able to provide teachers in training to accompany the class.

Transportation. Transportation need not be an issue in service learning. Ideally, a service learning project can be completed either at the school or within walking distance of it. Unfortunately, it is not always possible to service learn in or near the school. Figuring out how to transport an entire class of students to a service site may be one of the most difficult logistical tasks involved in off-campus service learning. Sometimes, parent volunteers can drive. Having students bring money for a bus ride is also a possibility, although some districts will not allow this. Some schools keep bus passes for such occasions. If a bus needs to be hired, then the class may need to raise $50–$150 to cover the cost.

FINAL REFLECTIONS

No experience having a meaning is possible without some element of thought. (Dewey 1916, p. 169)

Students do not learn from their experiences only. They must be given the opportunity to reflect upon their experiences. When a service learning project is complete, a final reflection provides students with the opportunity to tie together their service and classroom experiences. It also allows students to review the entire project and identify areas of growth. The academic aspect of the project should be highlighted in the final reflection. The final reflection allows the learning to take place while meeting individual needs of students. The final reflection connects all the components of service learning like pieces of a puzzle. Service and learning are the pieces linked together, and the picture of the puzzle is the result of the final reflection. Students are able to see the effects of their work when given the opportunity to reflect.

Part 3, the "toolkit," offers several options for final reflections, such as reflection summary and KWL. (An example of a completed KWL form appears in figure 2.6. A blank KWL form appears in part 3.)

Another option is to encourage students to write personal narratives about their service learning experience. The academic component of the service learning must be addressed in the narrative. One way to help students structure the narrative is to have them answer each of the following questions in paragraph form:

1. What did we do?

2. What was my part in the project? How did I feel about my part?

Sample KWL Chart

To be completed in three stages as the service project takes form and progresses.

K What we know.	**W** What we want to know.	**L** What we are learning.
Book Title: *It Takes a Village*	Community Connections	Service Learning Project: Babysitting Club
Kokou got lost. Yemi looked for Kokou. She was worried, but not afraid for him. Kokou got the things he needed to be safe and comfortable from the village. This village is a place where people look out for each other.	1. Who are the people in the community who help us? 2. How do we look for help in the community? 3. Who are the people in our community that need help? 4. What can we do to serve those who need help?	1. Parents, teachers, police, firefighters, doctors, nurses, babysitters . . . 2. Ask someone who knows where to find help, use the phone book, call 911 . . . 3. The elderly, the disabled, the sick, the young . . . 4. Served the young by starting a babysitting club for parents to use during school functions: Learned first aid in case of emergency. Learned how to care for those younger than ourselves. Learned new games, activities, and songs to help keep the children happy. Practiced keeping our patience.

Fig. 2.6. The KWL form summarizes what students Know, what they Want to know, and what they have Learned.

3. What did I learn?

4. How do I know that I made a difference?

A worksheet to guide students' reflections appears in part 3.

As a final step in the service learning project, distribute Reflective Evaluation forms to students. These forms help students individually internalize the service learning project. In addition these forms can be used to lead students into a group reflection.

REFERENCES

Cooper, J. D. 1993. *Literacy: Helping Children Construct Meaning*. Boston: Houghton Mifflin.

Cowen-Fletcher, Jane. 1994. *It Takes a Village*. New York: Scholastic.

Dewey, John. 1916. *Democracy and Education: An Introduction to the Philosophy of Education*. New York: Macmillan.

GOAL/QPC. 1992. *The Memory Jogger for Education*. Methuen, MA.

Gray, D. N.d. *San Diego Socratic Seminar*. Unpublished.

Routman, R. 1991. *Invitations: Changing as Teachers and Learners K–12*. Portsmouth, NH: Heinemann.

Part 2

Children's Literature: Springboards to Service

It Takes a Village ❖ The Giving Tree ❖ Now One Foot, Now the Other ❖ Smoky Night ❖ The Patchwork Quilt ❖ We Are All in the Dumps with Jack and Guy ❖ The Velveteen Rabbit ❖ Knots on a Counting Rope ❖ The Lorax ❖ The Hundred Penny Box ❖ A Taste of Blackberries ❖ Sadako and the Thousand Paper Cranes ❖ Stone Fox ❖ Sarah, Plain and Tall ❖ The Hundred Dresses ❖ The Switching Well ❖ The Trumpet of the Swan ❖ Dragonwings ❖ From the Mixed-Up Files of Mrs. Basil E. Frankweiler ❖ Roll of Thunder, Hear My Cry ❖ The Giver

It Takes a Village

Written and illustrated by Jane Cowen-Fletcher. New York: Scholastic, 1994.
Picture book. Primary–Intermediate grade levels.

Yemi feels very grown up when Mama asks her to watch Kokou, her little brother, at the busy market. Mama smiles because she knows that Yemi will not be looking after Kokou all by herself.

When Yemi stops at the market to buy some peanuts for her hungry brother, he disappears. All of Yemi's worries about her brother are taken care of by other villagers at the market. One vendor feeds him. Another gives him something to drink.

At last Yemi finds Kokou asleep on the mat vendor's mat. She thanks him and all the villagers who helped her take care of Kokou at the busy market.

Sure that Mama must be worried, Yemi hurries off to tell her what has happened. That is when Mama shares the wise saying that had been passed on to her, "It takes a village to raise a child."

Some important messages to gain from this book are:

❖ There is joy in helping others.

❖ Everyone contributes something important to the group.

❖ We need to be responsible for our actions.

❖ It's good to ask for help when we need it.

❖ *Thank you* are two very important words.

ACTIVITY BRIDGE TO SERVICE LEARNING

Look at the illustrations of the community in *It Takes a Village*. Ask students: How is this village like our community? How is this village different from our community?

List on the chalk board various places in the students' community.

Give each student a copy of the worksheet for *It Takes a Village* (page 35). Have students draw pictures of places in their community. Have students cut out their drawings and attach their community pictures to a large sheet of butcher paper or hang them on a bulletin board.

Follow up by discussing: How can we become involved in helping others in the different places in our community?

SUGGESTED SERVICE LEARNING PROJECTS

Establish class buddies with students in a younger or older class. Work together to plan a joint activity.

Start a school market to sell school supplies and items students make in class.

Form a babysitting club. Babysit during parent group meetings, conferences, and at other times when there is a need for babysitters at the school.

Have a food drive to collect food for the hungry.

Have a clothing drive to collect warm clothing for children.

Write thank-you letters to the people who have helped you.

RELATED LITERATURE

Golenbock, Peter. *Teammates*. San Diego: Harcourt Brace Jovanovich, 1990.

Mills, Lauren A. *Rag Coat*. Boston: Little, Brown, 1991.

Mochizuki, Ken. *Baseball Saved Us*. New York: Lee & Low, 1993.

Spier, Peter. *People*. Garden City, NY: Doubleday, 1980.

Stanley, Diane. *The Conversation Club*. New York: Aladdin Books, 1990.

DISCUSSION QUESTIONS AND VOCABULARY

1. What made Yemi feel grown up as she went to the market? (Mama asked Yemi to take care of her little brother. She carried him to the market.)

2. What can you do all by yourself that makes you feel grown up?

3. Why did Yemi stop to buy some peanuts? (She thought that Kokou was hungry.)

4. How do you think Yemi felt when she discovered her brother was gone?

5. What did Yemi worry about while she was looking for Kokou? (She worried that he was hungry, thirsty, frightened, hot, and tired.)

6. Who took care of Kokou's needs while Yemi was looking for him? (The people in the village took care of Kokou's needs.)

7. How do you think the mat vendor knew that Yemi was looking for her lost brother? (He may have heard her cry, and a lost boy was sleeping on his mats.)

8. What important thing did Yemi remember to do when she found her brother? (She thanked everyone for taking care of him.)

9. What important message did Mama pass down to her daughter, Yemi? (It takes a village to raise a child.)

10. What does the message "It takes a village to raise a child" mean to you?

villagers (2): the people who live in a village, which is smaller than a town

mangoes (2): a yellowish red tropical fruit

family compound (3): a fenced area that has many houses

vendors (7): people who sell things

restless (10): uneasy, continuous movement

It Takes a Village

1. What made Yemi feel grown up as she went to the market?

2. What can you do all by yourself that makes you feel grown up?

3. Why did Yemi stop to buy some peanuts?

4. How do you think Yemi felt when she discovered her brother was gone?

5. What did Yemi worry about while she was looking for Kokou?

6. Who took care of Kokou's needs while Yemi was looking for him?

7. How do you think the mat vendor knew that Yemi was looking for her lost brother?

8. What important thing did Yemi remember to do when she found her brother?

9. What important message did Mama pass down to her daughter, Yemi?

10. What does the message "It takes a village to raise a child" mean to you?

It Takes a Village
by Jane Cowen-Fletcher

Name _____

Draw a picture of a place in your village or community where you can go for help. Write the name of the place on the picture.

What makes this a special place in your community?

The Giving Tree

Written and illustrated by Shel Silverstein. New York: Harper & Row, 1964.
Picture book. Primary–Intermediate grade levels.

A tree who loves a boy tries to make him happy by giving him everything it is within her power to give.

The Giving Tree is easy to read and should be accessible to all students in the fourth through sixth grades. The pure and simple message of love, compassion, caring, and giving is an important one that students can enjoy over and over again. Shel Silverstein's simple illustrations enhance the message in the text.

Writing time can be used to write a paragraph about how students can give to others. Encourage "I think . . . because . . ." statements.

Some important messages to gain from this book are:

❖ Sometimes we can give too much to others and not think enough about ourselves.

❖ Love involves giving.

❖ People's needs change as they grow older.

Activity Bridge to Service Learning

The Giving Tree worksheet helps students begin to think about themselves as givers. Using the worksheet, students compare the ways they give to others to the things they receive from others.

Draw a tree with roots and branches on a large sheet of butcher paper. Ask students to suggest ways in which trees give to people. Record their responses near the branches of the tree.

Give each student a copy of *The Giving Tree* worksheet (page 39) to complete. Ask students: How can we give to our community? Would we receive anything in return? Is it OK to give without receiving anything?

Suggested Service Learning Projects

Students write a paragraph explaining what they can give or what kind of service they can provide to someone they love. Students serve alone or in groups by writing contracts, creating presentations, and keeping journals.

Develop a service project around the idea of consumption of natural resources, keeping in mind the central question, How much can the earth give?

RELATED LITERATURE

Irwin, Hadley. *What About Grandma?* New York: Atheneum, 1982.

Joose, Barbara. *Mama, Do You Love Me?* New York: Scholastic, 1991.

McBratney, Sam. *Guess How Much I Love You?* Cambridge: Candlewick Press, 1995.

Munsch, Robert. *Love You Forever.* Ontario: Firefly Books, 1990.

Rockwell, A. F. *Gift for a Gift.* New York: Parent's Magazine Press, 1974.

Wilheim, Hans. *I'll Always Love You.* New York: Crown Publishers, 1985.

Zolotow, Charlotte. *If You Listen.* New York: Harper & Row, 1980.

DISCUSSION QUESTIONS

1. Why would the tree give so much to the boy? (The tree gave out of love.)

2. What did the boy give to the tree? (He gave the tree someone to care about.)

3. How was the boy selfish? (He took everything from the tree.)

4. How can you give too much?

5. How can you give too little?

6. How did the boy's needs change during his lifetime? (The boy's needs became more complicated as he grew older.)

7. When were the boy's needs the most simple? (The boy's needs were simple when he was very young and very old.)

8. When was the tree the happiest? (The tree was happiest when the boy was very young and very old.)

9. Why was the tree happy in the end?

The Giving Tree

1. Why would the tree give so much to the boy?

2. What did the boy give to the tree?

3. How was the boy selfish?

4. How can you give too much?

5. How can you give too little?

6. How did the boy's needs change during his lifetime?

7. When were the boy's needs the most simple?

8. When was the tree the happiest?

9. Why was the tree happy in the end?

The Giving Tree
by Shel Silverstein

Name _____

Draw a tree with branches and roots. Next to the branches, write ways in which you give, like the tree. Next to the tree's roots, write the things that you need, as the boy did.

From *Reaching Out Through Reading.* © 1998 Carrie Sorby Duits and Adelle K. Dorman. Teacher Ideas Press. (800) 237-6124.

Now One Foot, Now the Other

Written and illustrated by Tomie dePaola. New York: Putnam, 1981.
Picture book. Primary–Intermediate grade levels.

Bob teaches his baby grandson, Bobby, to walk by holding his hands and saying, "Now one foot, now the other." They do many fun things together, such as building towers out of blocks, telling stories, and going to the amusement park on Bobby's birthday.

When Bob suffers a stroke, Bobby is afraid and confused. His grandfather can't move or talk. Now it's Bobby's turn to help Bob learn how to eat by himself and to talk. Bobby even teaches his grandfather to walk by saying "Now one foot, now the other."

Some important messages to gain from this book are:

❖ We can all be teachers.

❖ Encouragement can lead to success.

❖ We need to be thankful for the many teachers in our lives.

❖ Stories about our lives are interesting and fun to share.

ACTIVITY BRIDGE TO SERVICE LEARNING

Collect 4–6 shoes from various people and put them in a basket. Show the shoe collection to the class. Ask students, What does each shoe tell you about the person who wears it?

Share the illustrations of shoes in *Now One Foot, Now the Other*. Ask students: Grandfather's and Bobby's shoes tell you something about what they need. Look at their shoes. What do they tell you? List students' responses.

Extend the discussion by asking students, Who is someone in your community who may need help like grandfather and Bobby?

Have students complete the *Now One Foot, Now the Other* worksheet (page 43) and share the shoes they have drawn for people with needs.

SUGGESTED SERVICE LEARNING PROJECTS

Visit a local nursing home to play games, such as checkers and chess, with patients.

Host a game day with a younger class and teach them how to play games.

Establish a cross-age tutoring program with another class.

Adopt a grandparent or an elderly person in the community.

Write letters to grandparents.

RELATED LITERATURE

Ackerman, Karen. *Song and Dance Man*. New York: Scholastic, 1988.

Aliki. *The Two of Them*. New York: Greenwillow Books, 1979.

Blue, Rose. *Grandma Didn't Wave Back*. New York: Franklin Watts, 1972.

Cooney, Barbara. *Miss Rumphius*. New York: Viking, 1982.

Hamm, Diane Johnston. *Grandma Drives a Motor Bed*. Niles, IL: Albert Whitman, 1987.

Henriod, Lorraine. *Grandma's Wheelchair*. Niles, IL: Albert Whitman, 1982.

Hines, Anna Grossnickle. *Gramma's Walk*. New York: Greenwillow Books, 1993.

MacLachlan, Patricia. *Through Grandpa's Eyes*. New York: Harper & Row, 1980.

Stevens, Margaret. *When Grandpa Died*. Chicago: Children's Press, 1979.

Williams, Barbara. *Kevin's Grandma*. New York: E. P. Dutton, 1975.

DISCUSSION QUESTIONS AND VOCABULARY

1. What did Bob say to Bobby when he was learning to walk? ("Now one foot, now the other.")

2. What special things did Bobby do on his birthday? (He went to an amusement park, rode a roller coaster, had his picture taken with Bob, made a phonograph record, and watched fireworks with Bob.)

3. Describe your favorite birthday.

4. What happened to Bob? (He had a stroke.)

5. How do you know that Bobby was sad? (He didn't know what to do. He couldn't eat or sleep, and he looks sad in the illustrations.)

6. Why was Bobby afraid when his grandfather came home? (Bob didn't remember him. He just lay there. Bob sounded like a monster.)

7. How did Bob "talk" to Bobby? (Bob had a tear in his eye. He blinked, made a sound, and smiled.)

8. Have you ever "talked" to people without saying anything? How did you do it?

9. How did the book get its title? (Bobby told his grandfather, "Now one foot, now the other." These are the same words that Bob used to teach Bobby how to walk.)

10. What have you taught someone else to do? How did you feel?

amusement park: a park with rides, games, and food

roller coaster: an elevated railway with curves and inclines

phonograph record: a vinyl disk that carries recorded sounds; it can be played using a phonograph

stroke: a sudden interruption of the blood supply to the brain

recognize: to be able to identify someone or something previously known

shoulder: where the arm connects to the body

Now One Foot, Now the Other

1. What did Bob say to Bobby when he was learning to walk?

2. What special things did Bobby do on his birthday?

3. Describe your favorite birthday.

4. What happened to Bob?

5. How do you know that Bobby was sad?

6. Why was Bobby afraid when his grandfather came home?

7. How did Bob "talk" to Bobby?

8. Have you ever "talked" to people without saying anything? How did you do it?

9. How did the book get its title?

10. What have you taught someone else to do? How did you feel?

Now One Foot, Now the Other   Name _____

by Tomie dePaola

Try walking in another person's shoes.
Answer the following questions in the
space provided below.

Describe Grandfather. What does
Grandfather need?

Describe Bobby. What does he need?

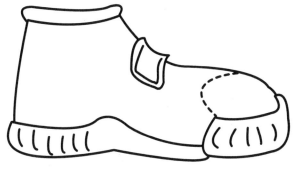

Color this shoe for fun!

Using the space below, draw a shoe that belongs to someone you know. Inside the shoe,
describe that person. What do they need?

Smoky Night

Written by Eve Bunting. Illustrated by David Diaz. San Diego: Harcourt Brace & Company, 1994.
Picture book. Primary–Intermediate grade levels.

After a riot, Daniel and his mother better understand their neighbors. When fire breaks out in their building, Daniel and his mother flee without their cat. After Daniel and his mother arrive at a shelter for victims of the riot, a fireman brings Daniel's cat, as well as a cat belonging to one of Daniel's neighbors, Mrs. Kim. Daniel makes an observation that encourages his mother to reach out to Mrs. Kim, who has been shunned because of her race.

Although *Smoky Night* is not challenging reading for most fourth or fifth graders, rediscovering the magic of picture books can delight students in these grades. This book and other picture books in the list of related literature can be used in a unit on picture books.

Some important messages to gain from this book are:

❖ Rioting affects the entire community, not just those involved.

❖ Differences between people shouldn't keep them from knowing each other.

ACTIVITY BRIDGE TO SERVICE LEARNING

Smoky Night is about personal growth. This activity stimulates students' thinking about this important topic.

Write a class collaborative poem called "I used to think . . . , but now I know. . . ." Each student should write their own response on a separate paper. Have each student share their response. Record the responses in a list to create the poem.

Give each student a copy of the *Smoky Night* worksheet (page 47). Ask students to think about the events that helped Daniel grow and change. Allow students to complete the worksheet with partners to encourage discussion about Daniel's personal growth.

Follow up with a discussion about catalysts to personal growth. Ask students: What events in your life have brought about changes in the way you think or see the world? What kind of events can you create to help change the lives of people less fortunate than you?

Suggested service learning projects

Write a short history of your life and share it in pairs or groups, emphasizing similarities and exploring differences.

Volunteer at a local shelter to raise money for the shelter, conduct a food drive, make decorations, do food preparations, help serve food, or help clean up shelter grounds.

Volunteer at an animal recovery center.

Related literature

Haley, Alex. *The Autobiography of Malcolm X*. New York: Ballantine Books, 1965.

Holland, Isabelle. *Now Is Not Too Late*. Toronto: Bantam Books, 1985.

Meyers, R. S., B. Banfield, and J. G. Colon, eds. *Embers: Stories for a Changing World*. Old Westbury, NY: Feminist Press, 1983.

Muse, Daphne, ed. *Prejudice: Stories About Hate, Ignorance, Transformation, and Revelation*. New York: Hyperion, 1995.

Discussion questions and vocabulary

1. What are some valuable lessons from this book? (People in a community can help each other in difficult times.)
2. Why didn't Daniel's family shop at Mrs. Kim's store? (Daniel's mom wanted to shop only at stores owned by African Americans.)
3. Why did Daniel's mom become friendly to Mrs. Kim? (His mom became friendly because of Daniel's comments about the cats.)
4. Why do people riot? (People riot because they are angry and frustrated.)
5. How do riots effect the community? (They hurt the community.)
6. Whom do riots hurt the most? (The people of the community are hurt the most.)
7. Are shelters always available for people who need them? (No.)
8. Why do you think this book is dedicated to "the peacekeepers"?
9. What does it mean to be a peacekeeper?

trailing: following at a distance

Reaching Out Through Reading Journal Reflections

Smoky Night

1. What are some valuable lessons from this book?

2. Why didn't Daniel's family shop at Mrs. Kim's store?

3. Why did Daniel's mom become friendly to Mrs. Kim?

4. Why do people riot?

5. How do riots effect the community?

6. Whom do riots hurt the most?

7. Are shelters always available for people who need them?

8. Why do you think this book is dedicated to "the peacekeepers"?

9. What does it mean to be a peacekeeper?

Smoky Night
by Eve Bunting

Name _____

Certain events in *Smoky Night* led Daniel to think about people differently. Use the blank spaces in the ladder to answer the questions about how Daniel changed.

How did Daniel's ideas about people change by the end of the story?

> Daniel at the end of the story:

> Event:

What events helped change the way Daniel thought about people?

> Event:

> Event:

What did Daniel think about people at the beginning of the story?

> Daniel at the beginning of the story:

The Patchwork Quilt

Written by Valerie Flournoy. Illustrated by Jerry Pinkney. New York: Dial Books for Young Readers, 1985.
Picture book. Primary–Intermediate grade levels.

Tanya learns from her grandma how the stories of a person's life can be represented or told in a quilt. Together, Tanya and Grandmother begin to make a quilt using fabrics that represent each member of the family. When Grandma becomes ill, Tanya decides to finish the quilt on her own. Before the quilt is completed, Tanya remembers to include the missing pieces of her grandma's life story.

Some important messages to gain from this book are:

❖ It is important to pass on family traditions and stories.

❖ We can help others in small ways.

❖ We should take time to remember the elderly.

❖ Quilts can tell stories about people's lives.

ACTIVITY BRIDGE TO SERVICE LEARNING

Display squares of construction paper. (Optional: Read *My Many Colored Days* by Dr. Seuss.)

Make a three-column chart on the board. Label the columns Color, Activity, and Feeling.

Ask students: When you look at the colors (indicate the construction paper squares), what activity do you think of doing? (Example: Blue might make someone think of waterskiing.) How does that make you feel?

Model for students how to take two colors to design a pattern that says something about the activity and feeling.

Distribute copies of *The Patchwork Quilt* worksheet (pages 51–52). Help students complete the worksheet activity. Follow up by brainstorming a list of feelings.

SUGGESTED SERVICE LEARNING PROJECTS

Collect fabric scraps to donate to a local community organization that makes blankets for the homeless.

Adopt an elderly person who lives at a local nursing home or belongs to the school community. Make a class quilt for the person you adopt.

Host Grandparents' Day at the school.

Perform a play or concert at a local nursing home.

Write stories or books for grandparents. Make quilted book covers.

RELATED LITERATURE

Guback, Georgia. *Luka's Quilt*. New York: Green-willow Books, 1994.

Hopkinson, Deborah. *Sweet Clara and the Freedom Quilt*. New York: Alfred A. Knopf, 1993.

Johnston, Tony. *The Quilt Story*. New York: Putnam, 1985.

Jonas, Ann. *The Quilt*. New York: Greenwillow Books, 1984.

Lyons, Mary. *Stitching Stars: The Story Quilts of Harriet Powers*. New York: Charles Scribner's Sons, 1993.

Mills, Lauren A. *The Rag Coat*. Boston: Little, Brown, 1991.

Polacco, Patricia. *The Keeping Quilt*. New York: Simon & Schuster, 1988.

Ringgold, Faith. *Dinner at Aunt Connie's House*. New York: Hyperion, 1993.

DISCUSSION QUESTIONS AND VOCABULARY

1. Where did Grandma get her scraps of material? (From the old clothes worn by each family member.)

2. How can a quilt tell your life story?

3. Describe the quilt on Grandma's bed. (It was old and worn, like Grandma.)

4. Describe a special project that you worked on with someone in your family.

5. Why was it such a special Christmas for everyone? (Grandma's family was together to celebrate the holiday.)

6. What pieces of fabric would you include in a quilt that tells your life story?

7. How did the whole family help with Grandma's masterpiece? (Tanya cut and joined squares. Mama sewed. Jim cut squares, and Ted helped Jim put them in piles.)

8. Why did Tanya quit working on the quilt? (She realized that Grandma was missing from the quilt.)

9. What was stitched on the corner square of the quilt? ("For Tanya, from your Mama and Grandma.")

10. Was it fair for the quilt to belong to Tanya? Why or why not?

restlessly: uneasily

anxious: worried

biscuits: quick bread made from rolled out dough

favorite: something that is treated with special favor or love

fabric: cloth

textures: the way things feel

absent-mindedly: lost in thought and unaware of one's surroundings

miserable: extreme unhappiness

plead: to argue a case or cause

questioningly: wonderingly

mischievous glint: a look that is full of mischief

delicately: carefully

The Patchwork Quilt

1. Where did Grandma get her scraps of material?

2. How can a quilt tell your life story?

3. Describe the quilt on Grandma's bed.

4. Describe a special project that you worked on with someone in your family.

5. Why was it such a special Christmas for everyone?

6. What pieces of fabric would you include in a quilt that tells your life story?

7. How did the whole family help with Grandma's masterpiece?

8. Why did Tanya quit working on the quilt?

9. What was stitched on the corner square of the quilt?

10. Was it fair for the quilt to belong to Tanya? Why or why not?

From *Reaching Out Through Reading*. © 1998 Carrie Sorby Duits and Adelle K. Dorman. Teacher Ideas Press. (800) 237-6124.

The Patchwork Quilt: Worksheet 1
by Valerie Flournoy

Name _____

You can use colors to show people what you are thinking and feeling.
For our class quilt, you will make four quilt squares using colors that you think match some events and feelings. Later,
we will put everyone's squares together to make our "Colors Talk" class quilt.
Use this chart to pick the colors for your quilt squares.

1. Write something that happened in the book.

What color matches that event?
How did that event make you feel?

What color matches your feeling?

2. Write something that happened in the book.

What color matches that event?
How did that event make you feel?

What color matches your feeling?

3. Write something that happened in the book.

What color matches that event?
How did that event make you feel?

What color matches your feeling?

4. Write something that happened in the book.

What color matches that event?
How did that event make you feel?

What color matches your feeling?

From *Reaching Out Through Reading*. © 1998 Carrie Sorby Duits and Adelle K. Dorman. Teacher Ideas Press. (800) 237-6124.

The Patchwork Quilt: Worksheet 2
by Valerie Flournoy

Name _____

Use the event and feeling colors you chose to create four quilt squares here. In Box 1 here, use the two colors you used to describe the event and feeling in Box 1 on Worksheet 1.

1.

2.

3.

4.

From *Reaching Out Through Reading*. © 1998 Carrie Sorby Duits and Adelle K. Dorman. Teacher Ideas Press. (800) 237-6124.

We Are All in the Dumps with Jack and Guy

Written and illustrated by Maurice Sendak. New York: Michael di Capua Books, 1993. Picture book. Primary–Intermediate grade levels.

Two rhymes are brought together as Maurice Sendak explores a central theme involving the homeless. Although this story, presented in a picture book format, does not require involved analysis by the reader, this tale has the potential to be interpreted as a critique of class structure, homelessness, family structure, community, struggles against inequity, and other prevalent social issues.

In the story, Jack and Guy struggle to rescue a helpless orphan. In the end, they find the child and decide to raise him together.

When first presenting this book to students, try first having students read the poem, and then look at the book. How do the pictures increase the level of understanding? What new information do students get from the pictures?

Some important messages to gain from this book are:

❖ The amount of money that you have doesn't define what kind of person you are.

❖ Caring makes a difference.

❖ When people work together, goals are easier to reach.

ACTIVITY BRIDGE TO SERVICE LEARNING

Ask students to explain what a symbol is. Record their answers.

Give each student a 3x5 card and instruct them to draw a symbol on the card. Have students show their symbols to the class. Encourage the class to guess the meaning of each symbol.

Give each student a copy of the *We Are All in the Dumps with Jack and Guy* worksheet (page 56) to complete in small groups.

Follow up by brainstorming events that have happened in your community and how people might feel during these events.

SUGGESTED SERVICE LEARNING PROJECTS

Have a representative from a homeless shelter or safehouse come in to talk about experiences. Have students brainstorm about how they can help.

Make an alphabet book using Sendak's drawings as inspiration. Donate the book to a younger grade.

Find someone in the school, such as a janitor or office staff, who is overburdened with work. Make a plan to help that person with his or her job.

Set up a big brother/big sister program with a cooperating class of younger students.

Have students write their own narrative dealing with issues such as homelessness, poverty, alcoholism, social classes, and similar topics. Publish the narratives in a school newspaper.

Have students write editorials for community education.

Related literature

Berck, Judith. *No Place to Be: Voices of Homeless Children*. Boston: Houghton Mifflin, 1992.

Bunting, Eve. *Fly Away Home*. New York: Clarion Books, 1991.

Johnson, Joan. *Kids Without Homes*. New York: Franklin Watts, 1991.

Marx, Doug. *The Homeless*. Vero Beach, FL: Rourke, 1990.

Voigt, Cynthia. *Dicey's Song*. New York: Atheneum, 1982.

Discussion questions and vocabulary

1. What is the story about? (Two homeless men who adopt an orphan.)

2. What does this story have to do with giving? (Jack and Guy give by taking care of the child, even though they haven't a lot to give.)

3. Describe Jack and Guy. Are they like people you know? (They are tough but caring. They are willing to take chances to help people in need.)

4. What do the rats symbolize? (The rats symbolize bureaucracy, wealth, greed, and power. They symbolize people who try to keep you from reaching your dreams. Discuss symbolism if students are unfamiliar with this concept.)

5. What do the kittens and the child symbolize? (Helplessness, need.)

6. What do Jack and Guy mean when they say that they will bring up the child as others do? (They will raise the orphan well, even though they are homeless themselves.)

rye: a cereal grain

orphanage: where children who don't have parents or guardians live

St. Paul's: a cathedral; in this story St. Paul's is an orphanage

trumps: the strongest suit in cards; the most powerful.

We Are All in the Dumps with Jack and Guy

1. What is the story about?

2. What does this story have to do with giving?

3. Describe Jack and Guy. Are they like people you know?

4. What do the rats symbolize?

5. What do the kittens and the child symbolize?

6. What do Jack and Guy mean when they say that they will bring up the child as others do?

From *Reaching Out Through Reading.* © 1998 Carrie Sorby Duits and Adelle K. Dorman. Teacher Ideas Press. (800) 237-6124.

We Are All in the Dumps with Jack and Guy

Name _____

by Maurice Sendak

Maurice Sendak includes many hidden messages and symbols (things that stand for something else) in this book. One example includes the line "For Diamonds Are Trumps." This means that money gives you power. Draw a picture of four more hidden messages or symbols in the book, and then write what Sendak might have meant by including them in the book.

Example:

For Diamonds Are Trumps = money gives you power.

_____

_____

1: _____

_____

_____

2: _____

_____

_____

3: _____

_____

_____

4: _____

_____

_____

The Velveteen Rabbit

Written by Margery Williams. Illustrated by Michael Hague. New York: Holt, Rinehart and Winston, 1983.
Picture book. Primary–Intermediate grade levels.

On Christmas morning a boy receives a stuffed rabbit in his stocking. The rabbit lives in the closet, forgotten by the boy who has more fun with his mechanical toys. The rabbit's friend, the Skin Horse, tells the rabbit that when toys are really loved by boys and girls, they become Real. The rabbit longs to be loved by the boy. He wants to become Real.

One night as the boy's nanny, Nana, is hurrying to find the boy a toy to sleep with, she grabs the Velveteen Rabbit from the closet. Soon the rabbit is one of the boy's favorite toys. When the boy becomes very ill with a fever, the Velveteen Rabbit is by his side.

Finally the boy becomes better, and the doctor orders the family to burn all the boy's toys, especially the Velveteen Rabbit. As the rabbit lies out in the rubbish to be burned, a lovely fairy from the garden kisses the Velveteen Rabbit on the nose and turns him into a real rabbit. The Velveteen Rabbit once again visits the boy in the garden. This time the Velveteen Rabbit is Real.

Some important messages to gain from this book are:

❖ Children who are ill need quiet care.

❖ Children who are ill, lonely, or afraid can find comfort in holding a stuffed animal.

❖ It is important to take good care of our toys and books.

❖ Good hygiene is important to prevent germs from spreading.

ACTIVITY BRIDGE TO SERVICE LEARNING

Invite students to bring one of their favorite toys to school for a Real Toy Day. Allow students to display their toys and share something they like to do with their toys.

Have students generate a list of activities that the boy in the story did with the Velveteen Rabbit. Then have students complete *The Velveteen Rabbit* worksheet (page 60).

Follow up with a discussion. Ask students: Why is it important to have a special toy? How do we help others when we give them a special toy?

SUGGESTED SERVICE LEARNING PROJECTS

Write letters to patients at a children's hospital.

Collect stuffed animals to give to a charity in the community.

Read rabbit stories to a kindergarten or first-grade class.

Make rag doll bunnies to give to patients at a nursing home.

Collect toys for a community holiday toy drive.

Make posters about basic hygiene rules to post in school bathrooms and classrooms.

RELATED LITERATURE

Birney, Betty. *Disney's Toy Story*. Racine, WI: Western Publishing Company, 1995.

Freeman, Don. *Corduroy*. New York: Viking, 1968.

Kroll, Steven. *The Hand-Me-Down Doll*. New York: Holiday House, 1983.

Polacco, Patricia. *The Trees of Dancing Goats*. New York: Simon & Schuster, 1996.

Rylant, Cynthia. *Henry and Mudge Get the Cold Shivers*. New York: Bradbury Press, 1989.

DISCUSSION QUESTIONS AND VOCABULARY

1. Describe how the Velveteen Rabbit felt about himself before he became Real. (He was shy and made of simple materials.)

2. According to the Skin Horse, what does it mean for a toy to become Real? (A toy becomes Real when it is loved.)

3. Do you have toys that are Real? Why would you say they are Real?

4. What did the boy and the Velveteen Rabbit do together? (They slept together, made burrows, had picnics, and took wheelbarrow rides.)

5. Do you have a toy that reminds you of the Velveteen Rabbit? What toy is it? Why does it remind you of the Velveteen Rabbit?

6. Why do you think the Velveteen Rabbit couldn't talk to the real bunnies in the yard?

7. What happened to the boy? (The boy became sick with a fever.)

8. How did it make the rabbit feel? (It made the rabbit feel needed.)

9. Why did the Velveteen Rabbit have to go out with the rubbish? (The germs of the fever had to be burned.)

10. How do you know the Velveteen Rabbit loved the boy as much as the rabbit himself was loved?

rubbish: trash

tissue: a soft piece of fabric used as a handkerchief

opportunity: a good chance to make progress

furry: covered with fur, the hairy coat of an animal

burrow: to make a tunnel in the ground

dingy: dirty

nightlight: a light that is kept burning through the night

mantelpiece: a shelf above a fireplace

splendid: showy, magnificent, grand

pincushion: a small cushion to stick pins or needles in to store them

nursery: a child's bedroom

bedclothes: blankets and sheets

butterflies: insects with bright, colorful wings

The Velveteen Rabbit

1. Describe how the Velveteen Rabbit felt about himself before he became Real.

2. According to the Skin Horse, what does it mean for a toy to become Real?

3. Do you have toys that are Real? Why would you say they are Real?

4. What did the boy and the Velveteen Rabbit do together?

5. Do you have a toy that reminds you of the Velveteen Rabbit? What toy is it? Why does it remind you of the Velveteen Rabbit?

6. Why do you think the Velveteen Rabbit couldn't talk to the real bunnies in the yard?

7. What happened to the boy?

8. How did it make the rabbit feel?

9. Why did the Velveteen Rabbit have to go out with the rubbish?

10. How do you know the Velveteen Rabbit loved the boy as much as the rabbit himself was loved?

From *Reaching Out Through Reading*. © 1998 Carrie Sorby Duits and Adelle K. Dorman. Teacher Ideas Press. (800) 237-6124.

The Velveteen Rabbit
by Margery Williams

Name _____

Follow the directions below.

How do you know the boy loved the Velveteen Rabbit?

Draw a picture of a toy in your room that is Real. Why did you pick that toy?

From *Reaching Out Through Reading.* © 1998 Carrie Sorby Duits and Adelle K. Dorman. Teacher Ideas Press. (800) 237-6124.

Knots on a Counting Rope

Written by Bill Martin Jr. and John Archambault. Illustrated by Ted Rand. New York: Henry Holt, 1987.
Picture book. Primary–Intermediate grade levels.

A blind Native American boy is told the story of his life by his grandfather. When the boy enters a horse race, the support he receives from his community helps the boy to feel like a winner (although he loses the race).

Some important messages to gain from this book are:

❖ There are ways to make dreams come true for the disabled.

❖ You don't have to come in first to be a winner.

❖ Family and history are important parts of our identity.

ACTIVITY BRIDGE TO SERVICE LEARNING

Tie knots on a piece of rope. Ask students to think about special events in their lives. Pass the rope around the classroom. As each student has a turn to hold the rope, they share an event in their life and how it made them feel. (Example: When my sister was born I felt proud.)

Give each student a copy of the *Knots on a Counting Rope* worksheet (page 64) to complete.

Follow up with a discussion about how events can create certain feelings. These events can help students understand needs in their community. For example, the event of moving into a nursing home might make an elderly person feel lonely. Losing your sight in an accident might make someone feel afraid. Students can then brainstorm service projects to change these feelings into ones of hope and happiness.

SUGGESTED SERVICE LEARNING PROJECTS

Have students pair up. Have one student in each pair wear a blindfold. Have the pairs go through an obstacle course or maze, working together. Research ways the disabled adapt. Raise funds to support an agency that works on behalf of the disabled.

Visit a home for the elderly and serve by reading, playing games, talking, or working on a project together.

Invite a guest speaker who helps to train the blind. Students can make informative posters for the school, letting other students know about how people who are blind adjust to the world and what students can do to help.

RELATED LITERATURE

Carter, Forrest. *The Education of Little Tree*. New York: Delacorte Press, 1976.

Jones, Ron. *The Acorn People*. New York: Bantam Doubleday Dell, 1996, 1976.

Meyer, Kathleen Allan. 1980. *Ishi: Last of His Tribe*. Minneapolis, MN: Dillon Press, 1980.

Tesman, Jean. *When the Road Ends*. New York: Avon Books, 1993.

Wood, Ted. *A Boy Becomes a Man at Wounded Knee*. New York: Walker, 1992.

DISCUSSION QUESTIONS AND VOCABULARY

1. What do you think of when you think of the disabled?

2. What made the boy an important part of his community? (Every piece counted in making the whole.)

3. How does his grandfather's story give the boy strength? (It reaffirms his ability to handle his disability.)

4. What does the boy's grandfather mean when he says, "Dark mountains are all around us"? (Everyone deals with different challenges.)

5. How was the boy able to overcome his blindness to ride the horses? (He used his other senses.) How do people in our culture deal with their disabilities? (They find ways to compensate.)

6. In what ways do you "trust your darkness"?

hogan: the Navaho Indian home; an earth-covered dwelling

frail: delicate

foal: baby horse

Knots on a Counting Rope

1. What do you think of when you think of the disabled?

2. What made the boy an important part of his community?

3. How did his grandfather's story give the boy strength?

4. What did the boy's grandfather mean when he said, "Dark mountains are all around us"?

5. How was the boy able to overcome his blindness to ride the horses? How do people in our culture deal with their disabilities?

6. In what ways do you "trust your darkness"?

Knots on a Counting Rope

Name _____

by Bill Martin Jr. and John Archambault

In the spaces below, write the events discussed in *Knots on a Counting Rope*. In the circles, write how the characters felt during each of these events. In between, write the names of the characters involved in the events.

Events	Characters	Feelings

The Lorax

Written and illustrated by Dr. Seuss. New York: Random House, 1971.
Picture book. Primary–Intermediate grade levels.

The Lorax tries to defend the environment as the Once-ler's greed for profit slowly destroys it. In the end, a boy is trusted by being given the last seed of a Truffala tree to plant.

Some important messages to gain from this book are:

❖ We have to be very careful with our environment.

❖ Greed can outweigh other's needs, but the Once-ler regretted his greed.

❖ Pollution affects everything around you.

❖ Individuals can make a difference.

ACTIVITY BRIDGE TO SERVICE LEARNING

This activity increases student understanding of environmental issues by exposing them to news articles. In addition, environmental concerns held by students will be exposed in the stories that they create. Both of these resources can be used as springboards into service learning projects by providing the class with information and providing the individual members of the class opportunities to write about the environmental concerns that they have.

Give students examples of daily newspapers or weekly student newspapers. Have students work in small groups to pick an article about the environment. Ask each group to share the title, problem, and (if possible) solution with the rest of the class. Allow each group to share their work. Give each student a copy of *The Lorax* worksheet (page 68) to complete. Follow up with a class discussion about new concerns students learned about by doing this activity.

SUGGESTED SERVICE LEARNING PROJECTS

Make an environmental wishing well and have students put in their wishes over the course of a couple of days. Type up the list of wishes and have students figure out practical ways to make these wishes come true. Let students vote on which wishes the class could pursue.

Have groups of students research environmentally friendly products for the school and make information sheets explaining what makes these products better. (To expand this activity, students may design their own environmentally friendly products and explain what makes them better.)

Conduct a neighborhood cleanup.

Have someone from a local park service come in to suggest ways students can help. Have students select one or more ideas to pursue.

Identify ecologically destructive businesses or businesses that are environmentally conscious and compare them in editorials written for a local newspaper.

RELATED LITERATURE

Burgess, Jeremey. *Endangered Earth*. Vero Beach, FL: Rourke, 1988.

Earthalert: The Active Environmental Game. Seattle, WA: Earthalert, n.d.

Green, Carol. *Caring for Our People*. Hillside, NJ: Enslow, 1991.

I Need the Earth and the Earth Needs Me. Detroit: General Motors, 1990. Videocassette.

Meadows, Graham. *Extinction Is Forever*. Auckland, NZ: Shortland, 1989.

Morrison, Meighan. *Long Live Earth*. New York: Scholastic, 1993.

DISCUSSION QUESTIONS

1. Does the Once-ler mean to hurt anything? (No. He is thinking too much about his profit to even think about how he is affecting the things around him.)

2. What does the Lorax want? (He wants the Once-ler to stop polluting and destroying the environment.) What does he do to get what he wants? (He brings the animals to the Once-ler to show him that he's driving them away.)

3. Discuss this quote:

    > UNLESS *someone like you*
    > *cares a whole awful lot,*
    > *nothing is going to get better.*
    > *It's not.*

4. How can an individual make a difference (positive or negative)?

5. What are thneeds? (They symbolize overindulgence.) What kinds of thneeds do we have, and how do they impact the environment?

Reaching Out Through Reading Journal Reflections

The Lorax

1. Does the Once-ler mean to hurt anything?

2. What does the Lorax want? What does he do to get what he wants?

3. Discuss this quote:

    > *UNLESS someone like you*
    > *cares a whole awful lot,*
    > *nothing is going to get better.*
    > *It's not.*

4. How can an individual make a difference (positive or negative)?

5. What are thneeds? What kinds of thneeds do we have, and how do they impact the environment?

The Lorax

by Dr. Seuss

Name _____

Clip words that deal with environmental problems from the newspaper. Use the clippings and your own words to write a newspaper story. Don't forget the title, the problem, and (if possible) a solution.

THE ENVIRONMENTAL WEEKLY
Volume 1 Number 1

The Hundred Penny Box

Sharon Bell Mathis. New York: Viking, 1975. 47 pages.
Intermediate grade levels.

Michael and his Aunt Dew have a strong relationship. Aunt Dew keeps a box filled with 100 pennies—one penny for each year she's been alive. Sometimes, Michael takes out the hundred penny box and counts out the pennies as his aunt reminisces about her life. Michael's mother wants to throw the old box away, but Aunt Dew tells Michael that when the box goes, her life goes with it. Michael struggles to make his mother understand the importance of the hundred penny box.

Some important messages to gain from this book are:

❖ It is important to remember family history.

❖ It is important to remember African-American history.

❖ Strong relationships can exist between the young and the old.

❖ Elderly people have dignity and rights.

❖ The young can learn from the elderly.

ACTIVITY BRIDGE TO SERVICE LEARNING

This activity allows students to create a record of their own history and someone else's history. This can help students understand the importance of personal history. Service learning projects can then be created around documenting the history of others in the community.

Model for students how to do a penny rubbing by putting a penny under a paper and rubbing the lead across the penny. Share an event from that year in your life.

Give each student a copy of *The Hundred Penny Box* worksheet (page 72). Students may work alone or in small groups to complete the worksheet. (If students wish to include family members' stories in their penny biographies, they will need to take the worksheet home.)

Use The Web to Service tool (page 191) to brainstorm service ideas using events from *The Hundred Penny Box*.

SUGGESTED SERVICE LEARNING PROJECTS

Correspond with elderly pen pals.

Write a penny biography of an elderly person and present it to him or her as a gift.

Volunteer to read aloud to patients in a nursing home.

RELATED LITERATURE

Duesing, Edward, ed. *America's Elderly: A Sourcebook*. New Brunswick, NJ: Center for Urban Policy Research, 1988.

Flournoy, Valerie. *The Patchwork Quilt*. New York: Dial Books for Young Readers, 1985.

Griffith, Helen. *Dream Meadow*. New York: Greenwillow Books, 1994.

Polacco, Patricia. *The Keeping Quilt*. New York: Simon & Schuster, 1988.

Seabrooke, Brenda. *Looking for Diamonds*. New York: Cobblehill Books, 1995.

Smith, Barbara. *Somewhere Just Beyond*. New York: Atheneum, 1993.

DISCUSSION QUESTIONS AND VOCABULARY

1. What kinds of service does Michael provide for Aunt Dew? (He keeps her company; he validates that she is still important; he gives her love.)

2. What kinds of service does Aunt Dew provide for Michael? (She tells him stories about his family history; she gives him love.)

3. Does Michael's mother care about Aunt Dew? Why or why not? (Michael's mother seems to care about Aunt Dew, but treats her like a child.)

4. Do you know an elderly person like Aunt Dew? What kind of help does that person need?

5. Why is it important for Aunt Dew to be able to keep the box? (The box symbolizes her life.)

6. Do you have anything that is as important to you as the hundred penny box is to Aunt Dew?

victrola (16): an old record player

britches (23): pants

Reconstruction (26): the process of rebuilding the South after the Civil War

Depression (26): a time during the 1930s when many people were extremely poor

irritable (33): crabby

mahogany (33): a type of wood

perspiration (38): sweat

cottonmouth (44): a type of snake

Reaching Out Through Reading Journal Reflections

The Hundred Penny Box

1. What kinds of service does Michael provide for Aunt Dew?

2. What kinds of service does Aunt Dew provide for Michael?

3. Does Michael's mother care about Aunt Dew? Why or why not?

4. Do you know an elderly person like Aunt Dew? What kind of help does that person need?

5. Why is it important for Aunt Dew to be able to keep the box?

6. Do you have anything that is as important to you as the hundred penny box is to Aunt Dew?

The Hundred Penny Box
by Sharon Bell Mathis

Name _____

Find some pennies from different years that you've been alive. In one of the spaces below, write down an important event from your life for one of these years. Next to the event, make a penny rubbing. Then ask a friend, a parent, a grandparent, or someone else that you know to recall an event from one of the years that you have pennies for. Write down their story next to a penny rubbing. (Directions for penny rubbing: Put your penny under the paper, centered in the square. Hold the penny in place. Use a pencil, and rub the lead over the penny to get a print.)

1. Event from your life: _____

_____

Someone else's story: _____

_____

2. Event from your life: _____

_____

Someone else's story: _____

_____

3. Event from your life: _____

_____

Someone else's story: _____

_____

4. Event from your life: _____

_____

Someone else's story: _____

_____

A Taste of Blackberries

Doris Buchanan Smith. Illustrated by Charles Robinson. New York: Scholastic, 1973.
73 pages.
Intermediate grade levels.

Jamie loves to play practical jokes and show off. So, when he is stung by a bee and taken away in an ambulance, his best friend doubts the seriousness of the event. However, Jamie, who is allergic to bee stings, dies. This story tells how his best friend copes with Jamie's death. He doesn't understand why Jamie had to die, and wonders whether he could have prevented it. Eventually he learns that some questions do not have answers. He realizes that Jamie's death is nobody's fault. At the end of the story, the boy brings a basket of blackberries to Jamie's mom. The boy knows in his heart that they are blackberries that he and Jamie would have picked together.

Some important messages to gain from this book are:

❖ One of the hardest things to learn is that some questions don't have answers.

❖ There are steps to accepting loss.

❖ Your work to accept death will help others, too.

❖ Treat every day as a special day.

❖ Be sensitive to others' feelings.

ACTIVITY BRIDGE TO SERVICE LEARNING

Prior to the activity, make an overhead of the *A Taste of Blackberries* worksheet (page 80).

Discuss with students the feelings we experience when someone close to us dies. Share the overhead to look at the categories of denial, guilt, anger, sadness, and acceptance.

As a group, have students share their definitions of each category and what a person might say to express that feeling.

Give each student a copy of the *A Taste of Blackberries* worksheet. Students work with a partner or in small groups to complete the activity.

On a large piece of butcher paper that is labeled with the five categories, have student groups record their quotes from the book.

Debrief the activity by sharing all the quotes from each category.

Follow up by asking students: What would help someone who is experiencing all these feelings after the loss of a loved one?

SUGGESTED SERVICE LEARNING PROJECTS

Visit a local cemetery and clean up litter.

Invite a guest speaker from a local hospice to talk to students about the hospice's work and projects that would support it.

Write sympathy notes to a family in the community who has recently lost a family member.

Contact a local hospital to identify a project that would support its work with grieving families.

RELATED LITERATURE

Bauer, Marion Dane. *On My Honor*. New York: Clarion Books, 1986.

dePaola, Tomie. *Nana Upstairs and Nana Downstairs*. New York: G. P. Putnam's Sons, 1973.

Hines, Anna Grossnickle. *Remember the Butterflies*. New York: Dutton Children's Books, 1991.

Miles, Miska. *Annie and the Old One*. Boston: Little, Brown, 1971.

Paterson, Katherine. *Bridge to Terabithia*. New York: Thomas Y. Crowell, 1977.

Paulsen, Gary. *Tracker*. Scarsdale, NY: Bradbury Press, 1984.

Powell, E. Sandy. *Geranium Morning*. Minneapolis, MN: Carolrhoda Books, 1990.

Viorst, Judith. *The Tenth Good Thing About Barney*. New York: Atheneum, 1971.

Zindel, Paul. *A Begonia for Miss Applebaum*. New York: Harper & Row, 1989.

DISCUSSION QUESTIONS AND VOCABULARY

Chapter 1

1. How do you know the boys were not supposed to be in the blackberry patch? (Others were talking about them.)

2. Why didn't the boys like Mrs. Houser? (It seemed she was looking out of the window so she could yell at them.)

3. What did Mrs. Houser want the boys to do? (She wanted them to collect Japanese beetles for her.)

4. Explain a time when you were nervous like the boys.

5. How do you feel about Jamie? Does he remind you of anyone?

thicket (1): a dense growth of small trees or bushes

crimson (4): a deep purple red

snitching (5): stealing

shinnied up (6): climbed

buoy (8): a floating marker

Chapter 2

1. Would you have helped Mrs. Houser? Why or why not?

2. Why did Jamie agree to help Mrs. Houser? (He would get to walk all over her lawn.)

3. Besides each other, who was one of the boys' best friend? (Heather was one of their best friends.)

4. What would you like to tell the boys about hitchhiking?

hoisted (17): lifted

suspicious (18): questionable

mimicked (19): imitated, copied

uncanniest (19): eeriest, most mysterious

Chapter 3

1. What happened to Jamie while they were scraping Japanese beetles off the grapevines? (He was stung by a bee.)

2. What was Jamie doing instead of collecting the beetles? (He was poking a bee hole.)

3. Where did the boy go when Jamie started his "act" on the lawn? Why? (He went to his own backyard to ignore Jamie.)

4. What would you have done?

5. Why do you think the boy went back to picking beetles after the ambulance took Jamie away?

attendant (27): one who accompanies someone or something

disgustedly (29): with distaste and anger

dirt daubs (29): little bits of dirt used for plastering

urgency (30): needing immediate attention

Chapter 4

1. How did the boy feel when Martha mentioned the "am-blance"? (He felt it was no big deal. It was another of Jamie's attention-getting acts.)

2. How did the boy feel when his mother told him what happened to Jamie? (He felt as if she punched him in the stomach.)

3. What did the boy do when he went up to his room? (He thought about Jamie.)

4. What would you have done?

5. Make a message in Morse code or another code for the boy.

conscience (32): a sense of moral goodness and conduct

Morse code (37): a code using dots and dashes for letters of the alphabet

Chapter 5

1. Why didn't the boy want to go to the funeral? (As long as he acted as if Jamie wasn't dead, he wouldn't be dead.)

2. Do you think the boy should have gone? Why or why not?

3. What went through the boy's mind when he saw Jamie? (It didn't look like Jamie when he slept. Jamie slept all bunched up.)

4. How did the boy feel when he ran out of the funeral parlor? (He was angry.)

5. Why do you think it was important that the boy saw his mother go into Jamie's house?

panicky (42): suddenly fearful   **scurried** (46): moved quickly, scampered

Chapter 6

1. Why did the boy go to Mrs. Mullins' garden? (It was the most private place he knew.)

2. When have you felt that the air was so empty that you had to say something?

3. Why was Mrs. Mullins sorry? (She was sorry for Jamie and the boy because she knew they were friends.)

4. What did Mrs. Mullins say about Jamie's death? (One of the hardest things to learn is that some questions don't have answers.)

5. What would you like to say to the boy?

timidly (50): without courage   **apparently** (55): seemingly
raggedy (52): worn out

Chapter 7

1. Why didn't the boy want to go to Jamie's house? (People would be crying. He wouldn't know what to say. It wouldn't be fair to remind Jamie's mother of Jamie.)

2. What made Jamie's death seem real? (His mother going back and forth and all the cars made it real.)

3. Describe a time when you talked to someone with just your eyes.

substitute (58): a person or thing that takes the place of another   **procession** (63): a group of people moving along in an organized way, like a parade

Chapter 8

1. What two things did the boy's father say Jamie would want him to do? (Jamie would want him to eat and smile.)

2. Why do you think it seemed important to the boy to pick blackberries?

3. Why did he need two baskets? (One was for him and the other for Jamie's mom.)

4. Why did it bother him that the kids were playing? (He thought they had forgotten Jamie.)

5. How did seeing Jamie's mom help the boy?

6. How did the boy show that he accepted Jamie's death? (He went out to play.)

7. Write a note to the boy. What can you say that might help him?

disloyal (66): not faithful   **hunched** (68): bent over
rummaged (67): searched

Reaching Out Through Reading Journal Reflections

A Taste of Blackberries

Chapters 1–2

1. How do you know the boys were not supposed to be in the blackberry patch?
2. Why didn't the boys like Mrs. Houser?
3. What did Mrs. Houser want the boys to do?
4. Explain a time when you were nervous like the boys.
5. How do you feel about Jamie? Does he remind you of anyone?
6. Would you have helped Mrs. Houser? Why or why not?
7. Why did Jamie agree to help Mrs. Houser?
8. Besides each other, who was the boys' best friend?
9. What would you like to tell the boys about hitchhiking?

Chapters 3–4

1. What happened to Jamie while they were scraping Japanese beetles off the grapevines?
2. What was Jamie doing instead of collecting the beetles?
3. Where did the boy go when Jamie started his "act" on the lawn? Why?
4. What would you have done?
5. Why do you think the boy went back to picking beetles after the ambulance took Jamie away?
6. How did the boy feel when Martha mentioned the "am-blance"?
7. How did the boy feel when his mother told him what happened to Jamie?
8. What did the boy do when he went up to his room?
9. What would you have done?
10. Make a message in Morse code or another code for the boy.

Chapters 5–6

1. Why didn't the boy want to go to the funeral?
2. Do you think the boy should have gone? Why or why not?
3. What went through the boy's mind when he saw Jamie?
4. How did the boy feel when he ran out of the funeral parlor?
5. Why do you think it was important that the boy saw his mother go into Jamie's house?
6. Why did the boy go to Mrs. Mullins' garden?
7. When have you felt that the air was so empty that you had to say something?
8. Why was Mrs. Mullins sorry?
9. What did Mrs. Mullins say about Jamie's death?
10. What would you like to say to the boy?

Chapters 7–8

1. Why didn't the boy want to go to Jamie's house?
2. What made Jamie's death seem real?
3. Describe a time when you talked to someone with just your eyes.
4. What two things did the boy's father say Jamie would want him to do?
5. Why do you think it seemed important to the boy to pick blackberries?
6. Why did he need two baskets?
7. Why did it bother him that the kids were playing?
8. How did seeing Jamie's mom help the boy?
9. How did the boy show that he accepted Jamie's death?
10. Write a note to the boy. What can you say that might help him?

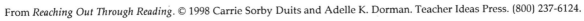

A Taste of Blackberries
by Doris Buchanan Smith

Name _____

Jamie's friend experienced many feelings after Jamie's death. In the circle, write a quote from the book to fit his feelings. Include the page number next to the quote.

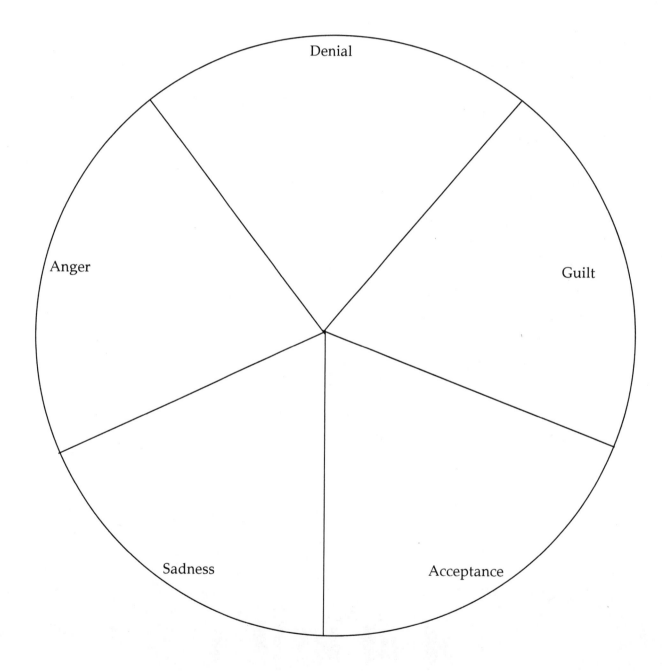

Sadako and the Thousand Paper Cranes

Eleanor Coerr. New York: Bantam Doubleday Dell, 1977. 64 pages.
Intermediate grade levels.

Ten years after the bomb was dropped on Hiroshima, an 11-year-old girl named Sadako contracts leukemia. Transformed from a lively, energetic child into a sick, pain-ridden patient, Sadako tries to get better by folding 1,000 paper cranes. She hopes that by folding 1,000 cranes, the legend of the thousand paper cranes will come true and she will get her wish to get well.

Some important messages to gain from this book are:

❖ Understanding people requires understanding what they are going through.

❖ It is important to include people who are different from us in our lives.

❖ Providing companionship to sick, lonely people can be extremely important.

❖ Hope is a special type of energy.

❖ War can continue to hurt people long after it ends.

ACTIVITY BRIDGE TO SERVICE LEARNING

Gather several different kinds of directories (for example, telephone directories, the *Encyclopedia of Associations* [Gale, annual]) for students to use during this activity.

Discuss the wide variety of efforts related to creating or keeping the peace. As a class, brainstorm what some of these efforts might be, and list organizations or keywords to help students find organizations working for peace.

Distribute a copy of the *Sadako and the Thousand Paper Cranes* worksheet (page 87) to each student. Help students complete the worksheet.

After students complete the worksheet, instruct them to cut out the information card at the bottom of the page. Also have them cut out the paper crane at the top of the page.

Collect the information cards. Alphabetize the cards and bind them to create a peacekeeping directory.

Organize students into small groups to create mobiles using their cranes. Display the mobiles in the classroom. Or, ask the school library media specialist to create a peace corner in the media center, where the directory and mobiles, along with books like *Sadako and the Thousand Paper Cranes,* can be displayed.

SUGGESTED SERVICE LEARNING PROJECTS

Service learning projects resulting from this reading might focus on helping the sick, the lonely, or people hurt by war; working for peace; or understanding various cultures. To increase the relevance of service learning projects, time them to coincide with World Peace Day (November 17) or Peace Day in Japan (August 6).

There are excellent educational sites related to Sadako on the Internet. One of these sites promotes the international Cranes for Peace project (http://www.he.net/~sparker/cranes.html).

If you do not have access to the Internet, you may obtain information from:

Hiroshima International Relations Organization
   A Thousand Cranes Peace Project Mailbox
   1-5 Nakajima-cho, Naka-ku
   Hiroshima 730 Japan

Hiroshima Peace Memorial Museum
   1-2 Nakajima-cho, Naka-ku
   Hiroshima 730 Japan

Sharon O'Connell
   2423 East Lake Rd.
   Skaneateles, NY 13152
   315-685-7078

Some local possibilities for service learning projects include:

Make paper lanterns or cranes for the sick or needy. (Directions for folding cranes may be found in the origami books and Internet sites suggested in the list of related literature.)

Research the atom bomb. Make a school newsletter to educate the school community about nuclear weapons.

Write editorials to be published in a local newspaper on the anniversaries of Hiroshima (August 6) and Nagasaki (August 8).

Make a temporary monument to commemorate a historical event the students choose. Select a symbol to make and leave at the monument, like the cranes in Japan. (Students might also wish to come up with an engraving like the one on Sadako's monument.)

RELATED LITERATURE

Bang, Molly. *The Paper Crane*. New York: Greenwillow Books, 1985.

Creech, Sharon. *Walk Two Moons*. New York: HarperCollins, 1994.

Kasahara, Kunihiko. *Origami Omnibus: Paper Folding for Everybody*. Tokyo: Japan Publications, 1988.

Krishner, Trudy. *Kathy's Hats: A Story of Hope*. Morton Grove, IL: Albert Whitman, 1992.

Maple, Marilyn. *On the Wings of a Butterfly: A Story About Life and Death*. Seattle, WA: Parenting Press, 1992.

Polacco, Patricia. *Pink and Say*. New York: Philomel, 1994.

Slote, Alfred. *Hang Tough, Paul Mather*. Philadelphia: J. B. Lippincott, 1973.

Yep, Laurence. *Hiroshima*. New York: Scholastic, 1995.

Internet Sites

Sadako's Garden: http://www.igc.apc.org/napf/sdkgarden.html

Sadako's Monument: http://www.yasuda-u.ac.jp/nagatuka/statue.html

Thousand Cranes Peace Project: http://hiroshima.ntt.jp/kokusai/hrjc/shusi-e.html

DISCUSSION QUESTIONS AND VOCABULARY

Chapter 1

1. What is Peace Day? (A day to remember the bombing of Hiroshima.)
2. Was Sadako being disrespectful when she called Peace Day a carnival? (Yes, although she didn't mean to be. Her family thought that this should be a day to honor the dead.)

leukemia (13): a form of cancer

tatami (14): a mat

Chapter 2

1. Why did Sadako try to ignore the pictures of the dead? (It is too painful, real, and scary.)
2. Why did she look away when she saw people with scars from the bombing? (She thought they were ugly, and she may have been frightened by them.)

Chapter 3

1. How would you feel if you started having dizzy spells like Sadako?

Chapter 4

1. Have you ever known anyone who was very sick? How did they feel? How did you feel?

throngs of people (27): lots of people

Chapter 5

1. What kind of service did Chizuko provide for Sadako? (She brought hope.)
2. What kind of service did Misahiro provide for Sadako? (He was helping her to believe.)

parasols (39): fancy umbrellas

Chapter 6

1. Have you ever lost hope or felt that you wouldn't get something you really wanted? How did it make you feel?

blood count (44): a measure of how healthy your blood is

Chapter 7

1. Have you ever had to comfort someone who was older than you? How did it make you feel?

Chapter 8

1. Why did Sadako's family bring her a silk kimono? (It symbolized hope; it made Sadako happy.)
2. What would you have told Sadako when she said, "When I die, will you put my favorite bean cakes on the alter for my spirit?"
3. Why didn't Sadako tell her family how much pain she was suffering the night they visited? (Their company meant a lot to her and to them. She didn't want them to worry.)

blood transfusions (56): injecting a person with "fresh" blood; used to clean the blood by replacing "old" blood with "new" blood

Chapter 9

1. At the beginning of the chapter, Sadako can no longer fold cranes. Why is this important? (Once she can no longer fold the cranes, she loses her hope of recovery.)
2. What do you think that it would be like to know you are going to die soon?
3. Why is Sadako still celebrated in Japan on Peace Day? (Her classmates chose to remember her by telling the world about her. The cranes have come to symbolize peace.)
4. At the end of the epilogue appears the following wish:

   This is our cry,
   this is our prayer;
   peace in the world.

   Why is this poem put at the base of Sadako's memorial? (Sadako died because there was a lack of peace.)
5. Make up your own wish in the form of a poem.

Reaching Out Through Reading Journal Reflections

Sadako and the Thousand Paper Cranes

Chapters 1–3

1. What is Peace Day?
2. Was Sadako being disrespectful when she called Peace Day a carnival?
3. Why did Sadako try to ignore the pictures of the dead?
4. Why did she look away when she saw people with scars from the bombing?
5. How would you feel if you got dizzy spells like Sadako?

Chapters 4–6

1. Have you ever known anyone who was very, very sick? What did they feel like? What did you feel like?
2. What kind of service did Chizuko provide for Sadako?
3. What kind of service did Misahiro provide for Sadako?
4. Have you ever lost hope or felt that you wouldn't get something you really wanted? How did it make you feel?

Chapters 7–9

1. Have you ever had to comfort someone who was older than you? How did it make you feel?
2. Why did Sadako's family bring her a silk kimono?
3. What would you have told Sadako when she said, "When I die, will you put my favorite bean cakes on the alter for my spirit?"
4. Why didn't Sadako tell her family how much pain she was suffering the night they visited?
5. At the beginning of the chapter, Sadako can no longer fold cranes. Why is this important?
6. What do you think that it would be like to know you are going to die soon?
7. Why is Sadako still celebrated in Japan on Peace Day?

8. At the end of the epilogue appears the following wish:

   This is our cry,
   this is our prayer;
   peace in the world.

   Why is this poem put at the base of Sadako's memorial?

9. Make up your own wish in the form of a poem.

From *Reaching Out Through Reading.* © 1998 Carrie Sorby Duits and Adelle K. Dorman. Teacher Ideas Press. (800) 237-6124.

Sadako and the Thousand Paper Cranes

by Eleanor Coerr

Name _____

Organization name: _____

Address: _____

Phone: _____

What it does: _____

_____

_____

_____

_____

_____

_____

Using the Internet or a reference book, research a peacekeeping organization. Write what you find out in the information card. Cut out the card. Write the name of the peacekeeping organization on the crane.

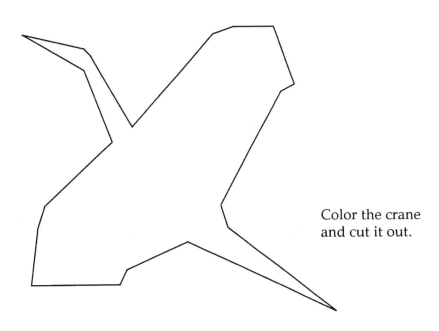

Color the crane and cut it out.

Stone Fox

John Reynolds Gardiner. Illustrated by Marcia Sewell. New York: Thomas Y. Crowell, 1980. 81 pages.
Intermediate grade levels.

Willy lives with his grandfather and faithful dog, Searchlight. When Grandfather becomes ill for mysterious reasons, Willy takes care of the farm and his sick, silent grandfather. Soon Willy learns about the back taxes that Grandfather owes the government. Willy is sure that paying off the taxes will restore Grandfather's health.

Willy enters a dogsled race. The prize is $500, just enough to pay Grandfather's debt. Willy risks all his savings to enter the race, and then learns that the notorious Stone Fox has also entered the race. Stone Fox has entered the race to earn money to buy land for Native Americans. They become enemies before the race. Near the end of the race, Searchlight collapses. Stone Fox is sensitive to the love that Willy has for his grandfather and his dog, so he stops the race. Willy carries his dog over the finish line and comes in first place.

Some important messages to gain from this book are:

❖ Asking a lot of questions will help you learn.

❖ Work hard and don't give up.

❖ Where there's a will, there's a way.

❖ Sometimes it is necessary to give up something important to get something else.

❖ Be considerate of others' situations, even when your own situation seems unfair.

ACTIVITY BRIDGE TO SERVICE LEARNING

On the board or on butcher paper, make two lists, one of student goals and one of personality traits.

Goals	Personality Traits
Learn to play the piano	Friendly
Read every day	Funny
Win my soccer game	Serious

The goals and personality traits do not need to match.

Draw a Venn diagram on the board and explain to students that this diagram helps us to organize and group information. Explain what each area of the diagram represents. Check to be sure all students understand the concept.

Next, ask students where they would put information that does not fit into any part of the diagram. Suggest that the area outside the Venn diagram can help us organize information—that's where we can put items that do not fit into any part of the diagram itself.

Tell students they are going to make a human Venn diagram.

Referring to the chart created at the beginning of the activity, select one goal and one personality trait to use in making the human Venn diagram.

If you can, go outside and draw a large Venn diagram (plus the extra circle) on the sidewalk or blacktop with chalk. Or, divide the classroom into four sections that correspond to the Venn diagram (plus the extra circle). If you are working in the classroom, you might be able to create the Venn diagram on the floor using string or tape.

Explain to students that:

Section 1 is for people who have the goal that is selected.

Section 2 is for people who have the personality trait that is selected.

Section 3 is for people who have both the goal and the personality trait that are selected.

Section 4 is for people who have neither the goal nor the personality trait selected.

Select one goal from the list and one personality trait. Students move to the section of the diagram that best describes them.

Have students move to the correct area of the room. Check for understanding.

Repeat the activity a few more times, selecting new goals and personality traits each time.

Give each student a copy of the *Stone Fox* worksheet (page 96). Model how to fill out the worksheet using one goal, personality trait, and situation from the story.

Allow students to work in small groups to complete the worksheet. Have students share their Venn diagrams with the whole class.

The Venn diagrams will lead to a discussion of service learning possibilities. Use The Web to Service tool (page 191) or the Reflective Windows tool (page 193) to generate more ideas for service learning projects.

Follow up with a discussion of how we can help others reach their goals. Ask students: How could we help people who face situations similar to the situation that Willy and Stone Fox faced, so that they might reach their goals?

SUGGESTED SERVICE LEARNING PROJECTS

Establish a school bank for students to deposit money into savings accounts.

Do errands for people in the community.

Adopt a patient in a nursing home. Send monthly cards and art work to the patient.

Establish pen pals at a Bureau of Indian Affairs school.

Grow potatoes. Give the potatoes to a local soup kitchen.

Organize relay races for a younger grade or a buddy class.

RELATED LITERATURE

Gill, Shelley. *Kiana's Iditarod*. Homer, AK: Paws IV Publishing, 1984.

Girion, Barbara. *Indian Summer*. New York: Scholastic, 1993.

Goble, Paul. *Dream Wolf*. New York: Bradbury Press, 1990.

Hobbs, Will. *Bearstone*. New York: Avon Books, 1991.

Maniatty, Taramesha. *Glory Trail*. Kansas City, MO: Landmark Editions, 1995.

O'Dell, Scott. *Black Star, Bright Dawn*. New York: Ballantine Books, 1990.

Standiford, Natalie. *The Bravest Dog Ever: The True Story of Balto*. New York: Houghton Mifflin, 1996.

Van Steenwyk, Elizabeth. *Three Dog Winter*. New York: Walker, 1987.

Wallace, Bill. *Red Dog*. New York: Pocket Books, 1987.

DISCUSSION QUESTIONS AND VOCABULARY

Chapter 1

1. Give two reasons why Willy's dog is named Searchlight. (She has a white spot on her head and she likes to lead the way.)

2. Name five things you know about Grandfather.

3. What is wrong with Grandfather, according to Doc Smith? (For some reason, he's given up on life.)

4. What do you think Willy should do to help Grandfather?

explanation (4): a statement that makes something understandable

Chapter 2

1. What promise does Willy make to Searchlight? Why? ("I won't ever give you away." They will stick together as a family even though Doc Smith said that Grandfather was going to die soon.)

2. How does Grandfather communicate with Willy? (Hand signals.)

3. How do you know that Searchlight is a special dog? (She knows songs on the harmonica. She knows when Grandfather is signaling with his hands. She understands Doc Smith's solutions to Willy's situation. She comes up with a solution for harvesting the potatoes.)

4. How are Searchlight and Willy like a team?

5. What do you think went through Willy's mind when Grandfather put his palm down at the end of chapter 2?

discovery (14): something learned for the first time

determined (18): having a fixed purpose or desire

hopeless (18): having no confidence to continue

Chapter 3

1. How does Grandfather feel about questions? (They are important for learning.)
2. What question would you like to ask one of the characters in the book?
3. Describe a typical winter day in Willy's life.
4. Grandfather used to say, "You're a good little worker and I'm proud of you." How is Willy proving his grandfather's words to be true?
5. Who do you think is waiting for Willy and Searchlight at the end of chapter 3? Why is he there?

errands (24): short trips to take care of specific tasks

forged ahead (28): kept going or moving

exhausted (29): extremely tired

impatiently (29): restlessly and eagerly

Chapter 4

1. Why do you think Clifford Snyder was afraid? How did he show he was afraid?
2. Why do you think chapter 4 is called "The Reason"?

derringer (30): pocket-sized pistol

Chapter 5

1. Grandfather used to say, "Where there's a will, there's a way." How does this thought help Willy now?
2. Willy asked Doc Smith a lot of questions. Choose one of the questions and answer it, giving your own opinion.
3. Mr. Foster told Willy to sell the farm to pay the taxes before he ended up with nothing. If he followed his advice, what would Willy have? (Nothing.)
4. If Willy could ask you for advice, what would you tell him?
5. Create a poster for the race in Jackson, Wyoming.

recommended (40): suggested

Samoyed (45): a breed of dog

Chapter 6

1. Why do you think Willy was so excited the second time he left the mayor's office?
2. What five words would best describe Willy the first time he met Stone Fox?
3. What was Stone Fox's dream? (Buy back the land that had been taken from his people.)
4. Now that you know about Stone Fox's dream, what five words would you use to describe Stone Fox?
5. How are Stone Fox and Willy alike? How are they different?

amateurs (47): those who lack experience or expertise

Chapter 7

1. How did Willy prove he is courageous, just as Lester told him?
2. How is Willy's situation similar to the Stone Fox's? (Willy is trying to keep from having his farm taken away and Stone Fox is trying to return the land to his people.)
3. What do you think Stone Fox is thinking as he tries to sleep in the barn that night?
4. Describe a time that you were so excited you couldn't sleep.

rooting for you (56): cheering for you, on your side

treacherous (57): having unknown dangers

courage (58): the strength to face danger

investigate (58): to search or inquire about

motionless (61): without movement

Chapter 8

1. Why do you think Stone Fox lacked the sparkle in his eyes that Willy remembered from before?
2. The anxious townspeople are described in chapter 8. What would you be doing on the day of the race? Where would you be? How would you feel? Who would you cheer for?

abrupt (63): sudden, without warning

contestants (65): the people competing in a contest

tension (68): strain

Chapter 9

1. What do you think Grandfather was thinking as he watched the race from his window?

2. How do Willy's and Stone Fox's racing tactics match their personalities? (Willy is a go-getter and Stone Fox is silent and steady.)

3. What do you predict will be the outcome of the race?

permitted (71): allowed

glimpse (73): a quick look

disqualified (71): not allowed to continue competing

effortlessly (74): easily

Chapter 10

1. What thoughts do you think went through Willy's mind as he crossed the finish line?

2. If Stone Fox could meet Grandfather, what do you think he would tell him?

3. Who do you believe is the real hero of this story?

victory (80): a win

Reaching Out Through Reading Journal Reflections

Stone Fox

Chapters 1–2

1. Give two reasons why Willy's dog is named Searchlight.
2. Name five things you know about Grandfather.
3. What is wrong with Grandfather, according to Doc Smith?
4. What do you think Willy should do to help Grandfather?
5. What promise does Willy make to Searchlight? Why?
6. How does Grandfather communicate with Willy?
7. How do you know that Searchlight is a special dog?
8. How are Searchlight and Willy like a team?
9. What do you think went through Willy's mind when Grandfather put his palm down at the end of chapter 2?

Chapters 3–4

1. How does Grandfather feel about questions?
2. What question would you like to ask one of the characters in the book?
3. Describe a typical winter day in Willy's life.
4. Grandfather used to say, "You're a good little worker and I'm proud of you." How is Willy proving his grandfather's words to be true?
5. Who do you think is waiting for Willy and Searchlight at the end of chapter 3? Why is he there?
6. Why do you think Clifford Snyder was afraid? How did he show he was afraid?
7. Why do you think chapter 4 is called "The Reason"?

Chapters 5–6

1. Grandfather used to say, "Where there's a will, there's a way." How does this thought help Willy now?
2. Willy asked Doc Smith a lot of questions. Choose one of the questions and answer it, giving your own opinion.
3. Mr. Foster told Willy to sell the farm to pay the taxes before he ended up with nothing. If he followed his advice, what would Willy have?
4. If Willy could ask you for advice, what would you tell him?
5. Create a poster for the race in Jackson, Wyoming.
6. Why do you think Willy was so excited the second time he left the mayor's office?
7. What five words would best describe Willy the first time he met Stone Fox?
8. What was Stone Fox's dream?
9. Now that you know about Stone Fox's dream, what five words would you use to describe Stone Fox?
10. How are Stone Fox and Willy alike? How are they different?

Chapters 7–8

1. How did Willy prove he is courageous, just as Lester told him?
2. How is Willy's situation similar to the Stone Fox's?
3. What do you think Stone Fox is thinking as he tries to sleep in the barn that night?
4. Describe a time that you were so excited you couldn't sleep.
5. Why do you think Stone Fox lacked the sparkle in his eyes that Willy remembered from before?
6. The anxious townspeople are described in chapter 8. What would you be doing on the day of the race? Where would you be? How would you feel? Who would you cheer for?

Chapters 9–10

1. What do you think Grandfather was thinking as he watched the race from his window?
2. How do Willy's and Stone Fox's racing tactics match their personalities?
3. What do you predict will be the outcome of the race?
4. What thoughts do you think went through Willy's mind as he crossed the finish line?
5. If Stone Fox could meet Grandfather, what do you think he would tell him?
6. Who do you believe is the real hero of this story?

From *Reaching Out Through Reading*. © 1998 Carrie Sorby Duits and Adelle K. Dorman. Teacher Ideas Press. (800) 237-6124.

Stone Fox
by John Reynolds Gardiner

Name _____

Using the Venn diagram below, describe Willy and Stone Fox—their personalities, goals, and situations. In the middle, write the things they have in common.

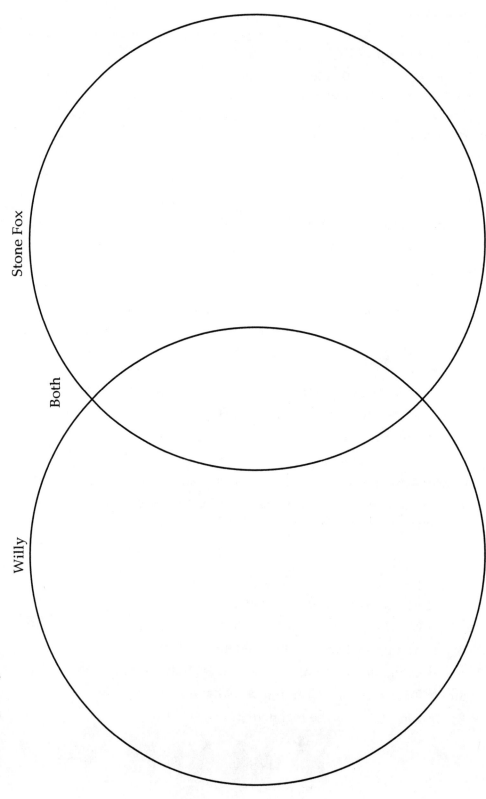

Willy

Both

Stone Fox

Sarah, Plain and Tall

Patricia MacLachlan. New York: Harper & Row, 1985. 58 pages. Intermediate grade levels.

Anna and Caleb eagerly await the arrival of tall, plain Sarah from Maine. Sarah has answered their father's advertisement to become his wife and stepmother of his children. Sarah has written to tell the family she is willing to meet them and stay for a while before deciding whether to accept the roles of wife and stepmother.

Sarah teaches the children about plants, animals, and the sea. Sarah even teaches them how to swim in the cow pond. Anna and Caleb learn to love Sarah very much, but does she love them? They anxiously look for signs that she will become their new mother. When Sarah learns to drive the wagon, they are sure she will leave forever. Sarah does leave, but she returns with gifts. She tells the children that she misses the sea, but she would miss them more if she left them to return to Maine.

Some important messages to gain from this book are:

❖ When we miss something, we realize its significance.

❖ There is always something to wish for and to miss.

❖ Even though we come from different cultures, we can learn from each other.

❖ There are many different kinds of families.

❖ Plants and animals are special gifts of nature.

❖ Caring for animals is an act of kindness.

ACTIVITY BRIDGE TO SERVICE LEARNING

Give students a 3-x-5-inch card and have the students record 10 of their favorite things on the card.

Collect the cards and mix them up. Redistribute the cards. Have the students circulate in the room to try to find the person whose favorite things appear on the card that they are holding.

Discuss how our favorite things say something about us. What favorite things lead to a service learning project? How can we share our favorite things with others?

SUGGESTED SERVICE LEARNING PROJECTS

Plant flowers or bulbs on the school grounds.

Have a fund raiser to collect money to donate to an orphanage.

Write letters to grandparents to learn about family histories. Use the information to write books for grandparents.

Invite a speaker from the local humane society to talk about pet care. Write plays about pet care to perform for younger students.

RELATED LITERATURE

Andrews, Julie. *Mandy*. New York: Harper & Row, 1971.

Burnett, Frances Hodgson. *The Secret Garden*. New York: Viking Kestrel, 1989.

Carlson, Natalie Savage. *A Grandmother for the Orphelines*. New York: Harper & Row, 1980.

MacLachlan, Patricia. *All the Places to Love*. New York: HarperCollins, 1994.

———. *Cassie Binegar*. New York: Harper & Row, 1982.

———. *Journey*. New York: Delacorte Press, 1991.

———. *Skylark*. New York: HarperCollins, 1994.

———. *Three Names*. New York: HarperCollins, 1991.

Montgomery, L. M. *Anne of Green Gables*. New York: Tempo Books, 1969.

Tripp, Valerie. *Changes for Samantha: A Winter Story*. Madison, WI: Pleasant Company, 1988.

DISCUSSION QUESTIONS AND VOCABULARY

Chapter 1

1. Why did Caleb want to hear the story of when he was born over and over again? (His mother died during childbirth, and he is curious about her.)

2. What is the story of your birth?

3. How did Anna feel about Caleb when he was a baby? (She thought he looked wretched and she blamed him for her mother's death.)

4. Why did Caleb want to sing? (He thinks he might remember his mama if he hears the songs she used to sing.)

5. What important letter did Papa share with the children? (It was Sarah's response to his advertisement for a bride.)

6. How do you feel about Papa's advertisement?

7. What question do you have for Sarah?

hearthstones (3): the stones in front of a fireplace

wretched (5): deplorably bad

homely (5): ugly

feisty (7): full of nervous energy

advertisement (8): a public notice used to acquire something

Chapter 2

1. Why do you think Anna wants a new mother?

2. Why do you think Caleb wants a new mother?

3. What are the three most important bits of information Sarah shares in her letters?

pesky (12): causing trouble

pitchfork (14): a long-handled tool with tines like a big fork, used for pitching hay

horse stalls (14): spaces in a barn or stable for horses

Chapter 3

1. List all the animals mentioned in this chapter. (Old Bess and Jack, gophers, woodchuck, sheep, cows, turtles, marsh hawk, dogs, Seal the cat, mice, a moon snail, gulls.) Why do you think the author included all the animals (and the different plants)?

2. What is the most important thing you learn about Sarah in this chapter?

3. What do you wish for Caleb and Anna?

Indian paintbrush (16): an orange and yellow flowering weed

Russian olive (19): a large shrub or small tree that grows in a dry climate

blue flax (21): a slender, tall plant with blue flowers

Chapter 4

1. How do you know that Anna hopes Sarah will become her new mother? (She hopes Sarah would be there when the roses bloomed in the summer and that there will be a wedding. Anna thinks she looks like Sarah's daughter.)

2. How do you think Sarah feels about Caleb?

3. Why is summer mentioned three times in this chapter?

scallop (22): a mollusk that has a ribbed shell

sea clam (22): an edible mollusk

oyster (22): an edible mollusk with an irregular shell

razor clam (22): a mollusk that has a long, narrow curved shell

conch shell (22): a large spiral-shelled mollusk

Chapter 5

1. How does Sarah show her love for animals? (She talks to animals and plays and runs with them. She names the lambs after her favorite aunts. She cries when pets die. She draws pictures of animals.)

2. How did Sarah get pictures to send to her brother William? What pictures did she believe were important to send to him? (She draws pictures of fields, sheep, the windmill, Papa, Caleb, and Anna.)

3. What were Caleb, Anna, and Sarah's first words? What was your first word? (Windmill and flower.)

4. How did Papa make a dune for Sarah? (The dune was a mound of hay covered with canvas.)

5. What do you think Caleb was thinking at the end of chapter 5? Why?

charcoal drawing (29): a drawing using a black carbon pencil

windmill (29): a wind-driven water pump

dune (29): a hill of sand that has been piled up by the wind

Chapter 6

1. List five things the children told Sarah about winter on the prairie. (It's cold. They go to school, but they stay home if there is too much snow. There is ice on the windows and Papa builds a fire. They bake biscuits, and they wear a lot of sweaters.)

2. Why do you think Sarah wanted to know about the winter?

3. What did Sarah teach the children? (How to float in the cow pond.)

4. When Anna slept that night, she said she was dreaming a perfect dream. The field had turned to a sea that gleamed like sun on glass. Why do you think Anna believed that dream was perfect?

cow pond (36): a watering hole for cattle

Chapter 7

1. Where did Sarah get the chickens? How did Anna know they would not be for eating? (From Matthew and Maggie. Sarah clucked at the chickens. They followed her around.)

2. Make a list of all the flowers mentioned in chapter 7. Draw a picture of one type of flower from your list. (Dandelions, summer roses, daisies, Rose and Violet [names], zinnias, marigolds, wild feverfew, dahlias, columbine, nasturtiums, tansy.)

3. Why do you think Maggie brought Sarah flowers?

4. Why did Sarah's eyes fill with tears? (Sarah was homesick.)

5. What important advice did Maggie give Sarah? (There are always things to miss, no matter where you are.)

6. What advice do you have for Sarah?

Chapter 8

1. Why did Sarah go out to the barn in overalls? (She wanted Papa to know that she was going to learn how to ride a horse.)

2. Why do you think Sarah wants to be able to go to town by herself?

3. What brought the family together in the barn? (A terrible storm.)

4. Caleb told Sarah, "Look what is missing from your drawing." What do you think he meant?

sly (45): clever and witty

stubbornly (45): refusing to give in

carpenter (46): a person who builds things out of wood

squall (47): a sudden, violent wind mixed with rain

eerie (48): frightening

Chapter 9

1. What made Caleb and Anna cry? (Watching Sarah learn how to ride Old Bess.)

2. What memory did Anna have of the wagon? (She had watched the wagon take her mother away.)

3. How do you think Anna felt as she watched Sarah leave?

4. What did Caleb worry about when Sarah was gone? (He worried that Sarah wouldn't come back because he was too loud and pesky and that the house was too small.)

5. What comforting message did Sarah tell Caleb and Anna? (She will always miss her home in Maine, but she would miss the children more.)

6. How did Sarah bring the sea to the children? (She brought them pencils that were the color of the sea: blue, gray and green.)

echoing (53): repeating a sound   **nudged** (55): gently pushed

Reaching Out Through Reading Journal Reflections

Sarah, Plain and Tall

Chapters 1–2

1. Why did Caleb want to hear the story of when he was born over and over again?
2. What is the story of your birth?
3. How did Anna feel about Caleb when he was a baby?
4. Why did Caleb want to sing?
5. What important letter did Papa share with the children?
6. How do you feel about Papa's advertisement?
7. What question do you have for Sarah?
8. Why do you think Anna wants a new mother?
9. Why do you think Caleb wants a new mother?
10. What are the three most important bits of information Sarah shares with the family in her letters?

Chapters 3–4

1. List all the animals mentioned in chapter 3. Why do you think the author included all the animals (and the different plants)?
2. What is the most important thing you learn about Sarah in chapter 3?
3. What do you wish for Caleb and Anna?
4. How do you know that Anna hopes Sarah will become her new mother?
5. How do you think Sarah feels about Caleb?
6. Why is summer mentioned three times in chapter 4?

Chapters 5–6

1. How does Sarah show her love for animals?
2. How did Sarah get pictures to send to her brother William? What pictures did she believe were important to send to him?

3. What were Caleb, Anna, and Sarah's first words? What was your first word?

4. How did Papa make a dune for Sarah?

5. What do you think Caleb was thinking at the end of chapter 5? Why?

6. List five things the children told Sarah about winter on the prairie.

7. Why do you think Sarah wanted to know about the winter?

8. What did Sarah teach the children?

9. When Anna slept that night, she said she was dreaming a perfect dream. The field had turned to a sea that gleamed like sun on glass. Why do you think Anna believed that dream was perfect?

Chapters 7–8

1. Where did Sarah get the chickens? How did Anna know they would not be for eating?

2. Make a list of all the flowers mentioned in chapter 7. Draw a picture of one type of flower from your list.

3. Why do you think Maggie brought Sarah flowers?

4. Why did Sarah's eyes fill with tears?

5. What important advice did Maggie give Sarah?

6. What advice do you have for Sarah?

7. Why did Sarah go out to the barn in overalls?

8. Why do you think Sarah wants to be able to go to town by herself?

9. What brought the family together in the barn?

10. Caleb told Sarah, "Look what is missing from your drawing." What do you think he meant?

Chapter 9

1. What made Caleb and Anna cry?

2. What memory did Anna have of the wagon?

3. How do you think Anna felt as she watched Sarah leave?

4. What did Caleb worry about when Sarah was gone?

5. What comforting message did Sarah tell Caleb and Anna?

6. How did Sarah bring the sea to the children?

From *Reaching Out Through Reading.* © 1998 Carrie Sorby Duits and Adelle K. Dorman. Teacher Ideas Press. (800) 237-6124.

Sarah, Plain and Tall

Name _____

by Patricia MacLachlan

Write each person's favorite things in the boxes.

Anna	Caleb

Sarah	Papa

Someone I Know	Me

The Hundred Dresses

Eleanor Estes. Illustrated by Louis Slobodkin. New York: Scholastic, 1944. 78 pages. Intermediate grade levels.

Wanda Petronski, a poor girl whose family is new to this country, claims to have 100 dresses in order to become accepted by the other girls in school. The girls tease her about her imaginary dresses because she wears the same faded blue dress to school every day. Peggy and Maddie, two girls in the school, turn the teasing into a daily game.

Wanda moves away, and nobody notices or seems to care. Her dad writes a note to the teacher to explain that they moved to the city, where they won't be teased because of their name and their heritage.

An annual school event is the November drawing contest. The teacher announces the winner of the dress drawing contest. It's Wanda! Her 100 dresses line the classroom walls. But it's too late for the girls to apologize for teasing Wanda, because she has already moved. Peggy and Maddie come up with a plan to let her know they're sorry.

Some important messages to gain from this book are:

❖ Teasing is cruel and hurtful.

❖ Once you've said something, you can't take it back.

❖ Try to understand what it's like to walk in someone else's shoes.

❖ When you've done something you regret, do everything you can to make amends.

❖ When you see something happening that you think is wrong, try to do something about it.

ACTIVITY BRIDGE TO SERVICE LEARNING

Arrange students in a circle. Have them retell the story of *The Hundred Dresses*. Each student should add to the last student's description of events. As the students are retelling the story, record the events on chart paper.

Assign small groups of students to role play (for the class) one of the events on the chart. After each group has role played an event, ask the students to talk about their feelings.

Give each student a copy of *The Hundred Dresses* worksheet (page 111) to complete. Follow up by asking students: How could we have made a difference for one of the characters in the book? Use the From Character Needs to Community Needs overhead (page 195) to discuss service learning possibilities.

SUGGESTED SERVICE LEARNING PROJECTS

Make a video to welcome new students to school.

Write letters to students who move away during the school year.

Host a classroom cultural fair for parents and grandparents.

Make a video about the school rules showing how feelings can get hurt when the rules are violated.

RELATED LITERATURE

Bunting, Eve. *How Many Days to America*. New York: Clarion Books, 1988.

Caseley, Judith. *Apple Pie and Onions*. New York: Greenwillow Books, 1987.

Cohen, Barbara. *Molly's Pilgrim*. New York: Lothrop, Lee & Shepard, 1983.

Danziger, Paula. *Amber Brown Is Not a Crayon*. New York: Putnam, 1994.

Freedman, Russell. *Immigrant Kids*. New York: Scholastic, 1980.

Hurwitz, Johanna. *Aldo Applesauce*. New York: Scholastic, 1979.

Porter, Connie Rose. *Addy Learns a Lesson: A School Story*. Middleton, WI: Pleasant Company, 1993.

———. *Addy Saves the Day: A Summer Story*. Middleton, WI: Pleasant Company, 1994.

DISCUSSION QUESTIONS AND VOCABULARY

Chapter 1

1. Why was Peggy popular? (She was pretty and she wore pretty clothes.)

2. How would you feel if you were Wanda?

3. If you were the teacher, what would you do to help Wanda?

popular (9): widely liked

entertainment (8): something that is amusing or fun

precarious (9): uncertain, insecure

Chapter 2

1. Why did the girls think that Boggins Heights was no place to live? (Old man Svenson lived there. There were only a few small houses in Boggins Heights.)

2. How did you get your name? What does your name mean?

3. What is "the dresses game"? (A group of girls waited before school to ask Wanda about her dresses. Wanda always said that she had a hundred dresses even though she wore the same dress every day.) What would you do if you saw someone playing such a "game"?

4. Describe Wanda, Maddie, and Peggy. Use five words to describe each girl.

5. What message would you like to give to each of the girls?

courteous (14): polite

incredulously (15): in an unbelievable manner

shrieks and peals of laughter (15): loud and wild laughter

laughed derisively (16): laughter to ridicule

cruel (18): mean and deliberately causing pain

embarrassed (19): feeling uneasy

Chapter 3

1. What do you think Wanda wanted when she joined the group of girls on that beautiful October day?

2. Describe a time when you wanted to be part of a group and you felt a little awkward.

3. Why do you think Wanda told the girls that she had 100 dresses?

4. What was the result of Wanda's comment about her 100 dresses? (They teased her.)

5. What could Maddie do about her feelings?

impatiently (22): restlessly

crimson (23): a deep, purple red

jaunty (25): carefree and self-confident

timid (28): shy, lacking self-confidence

enveloped in the group (29): surrounded by a group of people

stolidly (32): expressing little or no emotion

Chapter 4

1. Write a note to Peggy from Maddie.

2. What do you think about the coloring contest?

3. Why does Maddie think Peggy will win the contest? (Maddie thought Peggy could draw better than anyone because she was popular.)

uncomfortable thoughts (35): thoughts that make one feel uneasy

pretended admiration (38): false, insincere compliments

Chapter 5

1. What surprised you most about the drawing contest?

2. What did Wanda's father mean by "No more holler Polack"? (He didn't want his family to be teased anymore about being Polish.)

3. What was sad about the drawing contest? (Wanda had moved, and she would never know that she had won the drawing contest. The girls realized the truth about Wanda's beautiful hundred dresses.)

4. Why did Maddie think her actions were worse than Peggy's? (She could have said something to stop the teasing.)

5. How do Maddie and Peggy plan to make things better? (They decide to go to Boggins Heights to see if Wanda has moved yet.)

deliberately (45): intentionally

thoughtlessness (47): carelessness

unfortunate (47): unlucky

coward (47): one who has great fear

Chapter 6

1. Why was Maddie anxious to find Wanda? (Maddie wanted to be able to tell Wanda that she was sorry for teasing her.)

2. How was Wanda's house similar to Wanda? (The house and her dress were described as shabby but clean.)

3. How would you describe the girls' trip to Wanda's house? Did anything good come from their trip? (They discovered that Wanda had moved. The trip helped them understand Wanda better.)

4. What conclusion did Maddie come to that night? (She would never stand by and not say anything when someone was hurt or unhappy.)

5. What should the girls do next?

foreigner (51): someone from another country

consoled (51): helped someone feel better after a loss

make amends (55): improve or make something better

downcast (56): feeling low, down in spirit

discouraged (56): lost confidence

courage (58): the ability to face danger, fear, or troubles with confidence

disconsolate (60): downcast, dejected, cheerless

Chapter 7

1. How did Wanda show the girls that she received their letter? (Wanda wrote a letter to the teacher. She told the teacher which drawings to give to Peggy and Maddie.)

2. What helped "wipe away their tears"? (The girls realized that the pictures were of them wearing the dresses.)

3. What do you think was the biggest lesson that Maddie learned?

4. What message would you like to give to each of the three girls?

carefree (63): feeling free, without problems

ashamed (66): feeling guilty and regretful

Reaching Out Through Reading Journal Reflections

The Hundred Dresses

Chapters 1–2

1. Why was Peggy popular?
2. How would you feel if you were Wanda?
3. If you were the teacher, what would you do to help Wanda?
4. Why did the girls think that Boggins Heights was no place to live?
5. How did you get your name? What does your name mean?
6. What is "the dresses game"? What would you do if you saw someone playing such a "game"?
7. Describe Wanda, Maddie, and Peggy. Use five words to describe each girl.
8. What message would you like to give to each of the girls?

Chapters 3–4

1. What do you think Wanda wanted when she joined the group of girls on that beautiful October day?
2. Describe a time when you wanted to be part of a group and you felt a little awkward.
3. Why do you think Wanda told the girls that she had 100 dresses?
4. What was the result of Wanda's comment about her 100 dresses?
5. What could Maddie do about her feelings?
6. Write a note to Peggy from Maddie.
7. What do you think about the coloring contest?
8. Why does Maddie think Peggy will win the contest?

Chapters 5–6

1. What surprised you most about the drawing contest?
2. What did Wanda's father mean by "No more holler Polack"?
3. What was sad about the drawing contest?
4. Why did Maddie think her actions were worse than Peggy's?
5. How do Maddie and Peggy plan to make things better?
6. Why was Maddie anxious to find Wanda?
7. How was Wanda's house similar to Wanda?
8. How would you describe the girls' trip to Wanda's house? Did anything good come from their trip?
9. What conclusion did Maddie come to that night?
10. What should the girls do next?

Chapter 7

1. How did Wanda show the girls that she received their letter?
2. What helped "wipe away their tears"?
3. What do you think was the biggest lesson that Maddie learned?
4. What message would you like to give to each of the three girls?

The Hundred Dresses
by Eleanor Estes

Name _____

Pick a few events from the story and fill in the chart.

Page	Character	Describe the event	How did the character feel?

The Switching Well

Peni R. Griffin. New York: Puffin Books, 1993. 218 pages.
Intermediate grade levels.

The Switching Well is quality historical fiction. Amber lives in 1991, and Ada lives in 1891. One day, when Amber wishes that she lived 100 years earlier and, at the same time, Ada wishes that she lived 100 years in the future, they switch places. Over the course of one year, both Ada and Amber struggle to understand the different cultures they have joined. Together, they devise a plan to return to their own times.

The Switching Well is a challenging book for fifth and sixth graders due to its vocabulary. Griffin includes not only difficult words, but terms that are dated, due to the nature of the story. Many Spanish words appear throughout the text as well. Generally, students will be able to deduce the meaning of words relatively accurately within their given context.

Some important messages to gain from this book are:

❖ Over the last 100 years, attitudes have changed regarding minorities, women, religions, disabled people, and orphans.

❖ The grass isn't always greener on the other side.

❖ Drugs are not a new problem.

❖ Family and friends are important.

ACTIVITY BRIDGE TO SERVICE LEARNING

Give each student a piece of hard candy. Ask students to think about what they wish for others as they suck on the candy. Give each student a copy of *The Switching Well* worksheet (page 120) to record their wishes.

When students have completed recording their wishes, collect them in a box that you call the wishing well. Draw wishes out of the well to share with the whole class.

Follow up by asking students: What service learning project would be like a wish come true for someone in need?

SUGGESTED SERVICE LEARNING PROJECTS

Invite a disabled person to speak to the class. Discuss how various disabilities are similar and different. Ask the guest speaker how students can help disabled people in their community. Have students brainstorm additional ideas.

Invite an older African American citizen to speak to the class about racism. Ask the guest to address how issues of prejudice have and have not changed over his or her lifetime. Ask the guest speaker how students can help to reduce prejudice in their community. Have students brainstorm additional ideas.

How can the students help children at shelters? A guest speaker representing a family shelter could educate students and provide them with ideas.

Have students research the women's movement. An older woman could be invited to discuss how attitudes about women's abilities have changed. Have students discuss how they could raise awareness about sexism in their school.

RELATED LITERATURE

Allan, Mabel Esther. *The Mills Down Below*. New York: Dodd, Mead, 1981.

Brittain, Bill. *The Wish Giver: Three Tales of Coven Tree*. New York: Harper & Row, 1983.

Byars, Betsy Cromer. *The Pinballs*. New York: Harper & Row, 1977.

Koller, Jackie French. *If I Had One Wish—*. Boston: Little, Brown, 1991.

Lambert, Matthew. *Joey's Birthday Wish*. Austin, TX: Raintree Steck Vaughn, 1995.

DISCUSSION QUESTIONS AND VOCABULARY

Chapter 1

1. Why is Ada frustrated at the beginning of the story? (She is frustrated mostly by the sexism that exists in 1891.)
2. Is she right to be upset? Do these things upset you?

controversial (6): causing debate   **penalize** (6): punish

Chapter 2

1. What is the one thing you wish you could change in our world today?

exasperated (11): irritated

Chapter 3

1. After Ada travels into the future, she notices many things that are new or different from things that were familiar to her in 1891. What are some of the new or different things? (Cars, buildings, dress, people's behavior, money, cost of goods.)

indecently (19): not properly

indignant (19): filled with anger because of something unjust

cavalcades (20): parades

brusque (28): gruff

disreputable (28): untrustworthy

frock (28): dress

Chapter 4

1. Who is in more danger in her new surroundings, Amber or Ada? Why? (Ada is probably in more danger because she doesn't have the "street smarts" most people need to avoid dangers in 1991 America.)

cavorting (32): frolicking

uncouthness (34): rudeness

exasperated (35): frustrated

denial (35): refusal to admit something is true

Chapter 5

1. In a double-entry journal, respond to each of the following quotes from chapter 5:

    Passage 1: "Mamma would be furious if she knew that Ada had been put in with a person of color" (p. 44).

    Passage 2: "Violet was a big help, making Ada forget her conscience about playing with a colored girl— no, a black girl. Violet corrected her on that subject vigorously. Black was the proper word to use now. Since black had been slightly insulting in her day, Ada decided to avoid referring to the matter at all" (p. 53).

evade (46): trick

enlighten (46): explain

bewildered (47): confused

incoherently (48): not clearly connected

foe (52): enemy

vulgar (52): rude

humanity (52): humanness

conscience (53): known by your inner self

Chapter 6

1. Using a Venn diagram, chart the differences between the 1891 orphanage and the 1991 children's shelter.

2. In a double-entry journal, respond to this quote: "Amber realized that not only did all the kids wear the same clothes and have the same hairstyles, but they all had the same expressions on their faces. And their faces were all the same color. No Mexicans, no blacks, no Asians; not even any suntans" (p. 68).

3. Why aren't there any children of color at the orphanage? (The orphanage is segregated.)

glumly (59): sadly

seething (65): quietly angry

resolution (71): solution

Chapter 7

1. Have you ever made a wish that was really, really important but that didn't come true? Why didn't the wish come true? Was there anything that you could have done to make it come true?

2. Was it right for Ada and Violet to keep Amber's hair bow secret from Mrs. Burak?

3. Why doesn't Ada do well in history? (The history of the last 100 years is new to her.)

fretting (77): worrying

mellifluous (77): sweet sounding

heroin (79): a drug

heroine (79): a female hero

harried (81): hassled

delusional (82): hallucinating, imagining

imminent (84): about to happen

mirthless (86): without gladness

Chapter 8

1. Amber was whipped because of her determination to help Grof. Have you ever sacrificed in order to help someone else? What did you do?

2. Do you know anyone who is disabled? How are you and that person different from each other? How are you alike?

synagogue (90): a Jewish house of worship

congregation (90): a gathering of people

vigor (96): energy

impertinent (101): rude

Chapter 9

1. Why is it important for Ada to lie about her past? (If she doesn't, she might be put in a mental institution.)

2. Is it ever okay to tell a lie?

contemplating (105): thinking

anticipatory (106): relating to the expectation of an event

asylum (108): mental institution

temperance (111): moderateness

conviction (113): belief

drays (114): wagons

habitually (114): doing something over and over, as a matter of habit

reliance (114): trust with confidence

nattered (114): neatly

strode (115): walked with purpose

Chapter 10

1. Amber is planning to help Grof. What sorts of risks does she face? (She risks severe punishment from the orphanage, and she risks getting Grof in deeper trouble.)

laboriously (121): with hard work

submitting (121): surrendering

withstood (121): resisted

onslaughts (121): attacks

infirmary (124): where sick people go, like a hospital or clinic

benefactors (127): people who contribute money

epidemic (128): a sickness that many people get at the same time

endured (128): put up with

ingratitude (133): without thanks

verdict (134): judgment

Chapter 11

1. Ada was horrified when she read about Nazis in Amber's encyclopedia. Discuss a time when you learned about racism, sexism, ageism, or other form of prejudice. If you can't think of an example, ask your mother or father the same question, and write a summary of their response.

intricately (136): detailed

abruptly (137): shortly

dodge (140): move quickly to avoid something

resolutely (140): with determination

infallible (146): incapable of error

bigot (146): an active racist

dissolution (150): separation into parts

mauled (151): beaten

haven (151): safe place

Chapter 12

1. Why didn't Mr. Bauer think it was okay for Amber to have ridden Billy's father's bike? (Girls didn't ride bikes in 1891—it was considered unladylike.)

2. Has that sort of attitude changed over the last 100 years? Can you think of any ways that it hasn't changed?

Chapter 13

1. Why is the Little Old Lady in Tennis Shoes important? (She gives Ada a link to her own time.)
2. Why doesn't Old Mr. Burak want to return to Poland?

Chapter 14

1. How is drug use in 1891 different from drug use in 1991? (It is more prevalent in 1991. Also, in 1991 it is illegal to use many of the drugs that were used in 1891.)
2. How is divorce in 1891 different from divorce in 1991? (In 1891, divorce was uncommon.)

tartar (180): bitter person

serene (185): calm

Comanche (188): a Native American tribe

Chapter 15

1. Why has Violet kept her story a secret for so long? (It is dangerous to her family's well-being.) What is Violet's wish? (She wants to be reunited with her family.)

virtuously (192): sincerely

Chapter 16

1. Although the story has a happy ending, not all of the girls' problems are solved. Which problems have been solved, and which ones will Ada and Amber continue to struggle with? (Most notably, the problems of their times that existed in the beginning of the story remain unsolved.)

inadequate (206): not sufficient

adequate (206): sufficient

entreated (207): pled

consternation (209): confusion

con (211): cheat

conviction (214): belief

condolences (214): expressions of sympathy

vast impression (214): huge influence

entrust (215): to place trust in someone or something

incontestably (217): without argument

Reaching Out Through Reading Journal Reflections

The Switching Well

Chapters 1–5

1. Why is Ada frustrated at the beginning of the story?

2. Is she right to be upset? Do these things upset you?

3. What is the one thing you wish you could change in our world today?

4. After Ada travels into the future, she notices many things that are new or different from things that were familiar to her in 1891. What are some of the new or different things?

5. Who is in more danger in her new surroundings, Amber or Ada? Why?

6. In a double-entry journal, respond to each of the following quotes from chapter 5:

   Passage 1: "Mamma would be furious if she knew that Ada had been put in with a person of color" (p. 44).

   Passage 2: "Violet was a big help, making Ada forget her conscience about playing with a colored girl—no, a black girl. Violet corrected her on that subject vigorously. Black was the proper word to use now. Since black had been slightly insulting in her day, Ada decided to avoid referring to the matter at all" (p. 53).

Chapters 6–7

1. Using a Venn diagram, chart the differences between the 1891 orphanage and the 1991 children's shelter.

2. In a double-entry journal, respond to this quote: "Amber realized that not only did all the kids wear the same clothes and have the same hairstyles, but they all had the same expressions on their faces. And their faces were all the same color. No Mexicans, no blacks, no Asians; not even any suntans" (p. 68).

3. Why aren't there any children of color at the orphanage?

4. Have you ever made a wish that was really, really important but that didn't come true? Why didn't the wish come true? Was there anything that you could have done to make it come true?

5. Was it right for Ada and Violet to keep Amber's hair bow secret from Mrs. Burak?

6. Why doesn't Ada do well in history?

Chapters 8–10

1. Amber was whipped because of her determination to help Grof. Have you ever sacrificed in order to help someone else? What did you do?

2. Do you know anyone who is disabled? How are you and that person different from each other? How are you alike?

3. Why is it important for Ada to lie about her past?

4. Is it ever okay to tell a lie?

5. Amber is planning to help Grof. What sorts of risks does she face?

Chapter 11

1. Ada was horrified when she read about Nazis in Amber's encyclopedia. Discuss a time when you learned about racism, sexism, ageism, or other form of prejudice. If you can't think of an example, ask your mother or father the same question, and write a summary of their response.

Chapters 12–13

1. Why didn't Mr. Bauer think it was okay for Amber to have ridden Billy's father's bike?

2. Has that sort of attitude changed over the last 100 years? Can you think of any ways that it hasn't changed?

3. Why is the Little Old Lady in Tennis Shoes important?

4. Why doesn't Old Mr. Burak want to return to Poland?

Chapters 14–16

1. How is drug use in 1891 different from drug use in 1991?

2. How is divorce in 1891 different from divorce in 1991?

3. Why has Violet kept her story a secret for so long? What is Violet's wish?

4. Although the story has a happy ending, not all of the girls' problems are solved. Which problems have been solved, and which ones will Ada and Amber continue to struggle with?

From *Reaching Out Through Reading.* © 1998 Carrie Sorby Duits and Adelle K. Dorman. Teacher Ideas Press. (800) 237-6124.

The Switching Well
by Peni R. Griffin

Name _____

Inside the candy, write something you wish for and why you would like your wish to come true. Then, write a wish you would like to give someone else and why you want that wish to come true. When you are finished, cut out the candy wishes and put them in the wishing well.

My Wish for Me

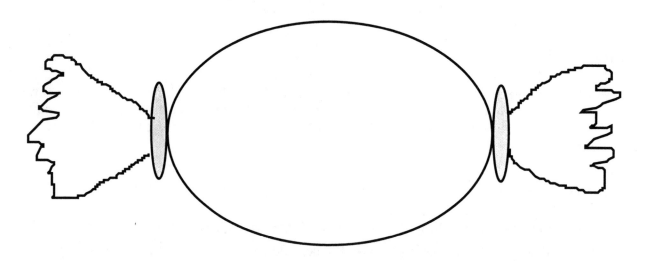

My Wish for Someone Else

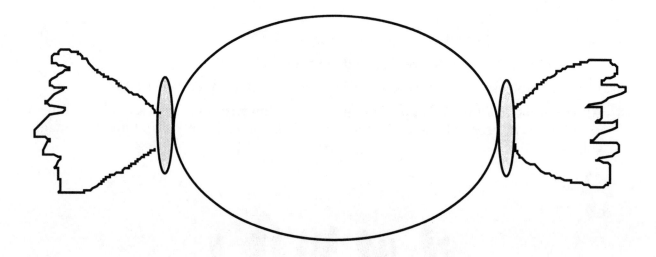

The Trumpet of the Swan

E. B. White. Illustrated by Edward Fascino. New York: Scholastic, 1970. 210 pages. Intermediate grade levels.

Sam Beaver befriends a trumpeter swan, Louis, who cannot trumpet. After Louis learns to read and write, he realizes he still can't communicate with other swans. Louis's father, the cob, steals a trumpet from a music store for his son. The cob agonizes over the loss of his honor and pride, so Louis makes it his mission to repay the owner of the store by earning money with his new trumpet.

Louis works at a summer camp, for the swan boats in Boston Common, and in a Philadelphia nightclub. In each situation, Louis encounters problems because he is different. In the end, Louis returns to his family to restore his father's honor.

When Louis does return, he brings his new wife, Serena, a beautiful trumpeter swan. Throughout the book, Sam Beaver helps Louis solve his many problems. He saves Louis's life in both the beginning and the end of the book. Sam Beaver is Louis's true friend throughout the story.

Some important messages to gain from this book are:

❖ Friends are loyal, and they find ways to help each other.

❖ Being different makes us special.

❖ Respect is a part of friendship.

❖ Pride and honor are important to everyone.

❖ We need to work through our problems.

❖ Prejudice is hurtful.

❖ Endangered animals need special protection.

ACTIVITY BRIDGE TO SERVICE LEARNING

Have students sit in a circle. Play Pass the Prop. To play, students pass a prop from the story as they share their thoughts about the story. (A prop for *The Trumpet of the Swan* might be a feather, trumpet, moneybag, or diary.) The student holding the prop shares, then passes the prop to someone else in the circle. The teacher begins with a sentence starter. Use the following sentence starters for *The Trumpet of the Swan*.

My favorite job Louis held was _____ because . . .

My favorite character in this book was _____ because . . .

If I were Louis, I would have . . .

I felt _____ when . . .

Give each student a copy of *The Trumpet of the Swan* worksheet (page 134) to complete.

Follow up by using the Web to Service or Three-Column Brainstorming overheads (part 3) to discuss possible service learning projects related to the book.

SUGGESTED SERVICE LEARNING PROJECTS

1. Make a class donation to the Audubon Society.

2. Adopt an animal at the zoo.

3. Study endangered animals and raise money to contribute to a group that supports such animals.

4. Study careers and work with volunteers in the community who would serve as mentors for students.

5. Identify jobs students can perform to help take care of their school. Have students apply for the various jobs. Each month, select different students to do the jobs. Jobs may include emptying the trash, dusting, sweeping, working in the lunchroom, and so forth.

RELATED LITERATURE

Coldrey, Jennifer. *The Swan on the Lake*. Milwaukee: G. Stevens, 1987.

Litchfield, Ada B. *Making Room for Uncle Joe*. Niles, IL: Albert Whitman, 1984.

Riskind, Mary. *Apple Is My Sign*. Boston: Houghton Mifflin, 1981.

Simon, Norma. *Why Am I Different?* Niles, IL: Albert Whitman, 1976.

Sobol, Harriet Langsam. *My Brother Steven Is Retarded*. New York: Macmillan, 1977.

Spier, Peter. *People*. Garden City, NY: Doubleday, 1980.

Wexo, John Bonnett. *Ducks, Geese, & Swans*. San Diego, CA: Wildlife Education, 1984.

Yashima, Taro. *Crow Boy*. New York: Penguin Books, 1985.

DISCUSSION QUESTIONS AND VOCABULARY

Chapter 1

1. Why was Sam reluctant to tell his father about his discovery? (Sam liked to keep things to himself. His dad might follow him. His dad might not let him go back to the nest.)

2. Tell about one thing you discovered by reading this chapter.

boggy (1): swampy

trudged (2): walked in a heavy-footed way

sly (3): clever, cunning

cygnets (6): baby swans

Chapter 2

1. Why was the nesting place perfect?
2. Describe your favorite place.

vixen (8): a female fox

investigate (10): to look carefully

convenient (11): easy to reach, suited to one's purpose

majestically (11): dignified, kingly

cob (12): a male swan

gander (12): a male goose

Chapter 3

1. Why did the female swan feel uneasy as she sat on her nest? (She thought she was being watched.)
2. How did Sam save the day for the swan? (Sam threw a stick at the fox and saved the swan.)
3. Describe the cob.

peered (15): looked intently

idyllic spot (16): a peaceful place

mysterious (23): curious

Chapter 4

1. Describe how the cob felt about fatherhood.
2. What makes you feel proud?
3. What are some of the dangers of the pond according to the cob? (According to the cob, the fox, skunks, otters, lead pellets, and coyotes are dangers.)
4. What dangers do children face today?
5. How did the fifth cygnet greet Sam? (He untied Sam's shoe.)
6. Why do you think the fifth cygnet greeted Sam that way?

poetical (26): creative and expressive

commonsense remark (26): a statement that makes sense

patience (27): waiting for a long time without complaint

protectively (31): doing something in a way that prevents harm or damage

Chapter 5

1. What was different about Louis? (Louis couldn't make sounds.)
2. Why did this difference concern his mother? (She worried that Louis wouldn't find a mate.)
3. The cob told Louis there may be some slight advantage in not being able to say anything. What was that advantage? (Louis could become a good listener.)
4. If you were one of Louis's brothers or sisters, what would you say to try to help him?

defective (36): lacking normal development
revelation (36): an act of showing
distressing (36): troubling, causing worry

vanity (37): pride
confine (39): to restrict

Chapter 6

1. How would the cygnets use their knowledge of flying? (They would soon be flying south for the winter.)
2. What are the three parts of flying? (The three parts of flying are taking off, ascending, and leveling off.)
3. What would it be like to fly like a swan?

marvelous (44): wonderful
attitude (46): emotional behavior to facts or conditions
exhibition flight (47): a flight that is a display for others

frenzy (47): wild excitement
elevated (47): raised or placed above

Chapter 7

1. What do you think about Louis's decision to learn to read and write?
2. The game warden complimented Sam and his father. What is one compliment someone has given to you?
3. What did Mrs. Hammerbotham think of having Louis in class? (At first she thought it was ridiculous, and then she was proud of herself.)
4. How would you feel about having a swan in class?
5. How would you help Louis?

compliment (57): praise
communicate (58): to make known, to exchange thoughts and ideas
sternly (60): strictly

catastrophe (60): a grave and sudden calamity
abandoned (64): given up without intent to regain

Chapter 8

1. What feelings did Louis and his family have when Louis returned to Red Rock Lake? (They were frustrated because they still couldn't communicate.)

2. How did Louis's love for Serena present a problem for Louis? (Louis couldn't tell Serena that he loved her.)

3. How would you feel if you couldn't communicate with your family?

4. What do you think Louis should do next?

5. What was the cob's idea to help Louis? (The cob wanted to get Louis a trumpet.)

6. How do you think the cob will get the trumpet for Louis?

disinclined (65): unwilling, reluctant

impatiently (66): restlessly

peculiar (67): something not ordinary

failure (68): lacking success

prolong (69): to lengthen or extend

sorrowfully (69): sadly expressed

coy (71): playful reluctance

desperation (72): extreme action resulting from despair

Chapter 9

1. How did the cob get the trumpet? How did he feel afterward? (The cob went through a store window to steal the trumpet for Louis. He felt like a thief.)

2. What did the cob sacrifice to get the trumpet? (The cob sacrificed his pride and honor.)

3. Have you ever sacrificed something for someone else? Explain your answer.

4. Write a newspaper headline and article about the incident.

antics (76): odd gestures or pranks

quest (76): a search for something

anxiously (81): feeling uneasy, full of worry

sacrifice (82): giving up something of value for someone else

Chapter 10

1. How did Sam help Louis? (Sam helped him with lessons and books. Sam helped Louis find a job.)

2. If you have gone to summer camp, describe how you felt when you were packing to go. If you have never been to camp, how do you think you would feel?

3. If you were going to camp tomorrow, what are the five most important things you would take with you?

possessions (87): things that are owned

taps (88): bugle call at night

reveille (88): bugle call in the morning to awaken people

duffel bag (89): large cloth bag used as a suitcase

Chapter 11

1. How did the boys at Camp Kookooskoos receive Louis? (They were anxious to meet Louis.)

2. How do you feel about Applegate?

3. According to Mr. Brickle, why was the camp called Kookooskoos? (It was named after the Great Horned Owl.)

4. What do you think would be a good name for a camp?

5. What does respect mean to you?

stern (93): the rear end of a boat

salary (94): pay for doing a job

prejudices (95): strong feelings formed before obtaining facts and developing understanding

celebrated (96): famous

Chapter 12

1. Why were the boys teasing Applegate, and what was the result? (The boys teased Applegate about his name. Applegate went out in a canoe on his own.)

2. How did Louis become the most distinguished counselor at camp? (Louis rescued Applegate.)

3. How do you think Louis felt when Applegate said he still didn't like birds?

4. What do you wish you could tell Applegate? What do you wish you could tell Louis?

5. What do you think Louis will wear around his neck next?

impractical (102): unwise, foolish

congratulations (103): expressions of joy or pleasure due to success

malodorous (103): bad smelling

megaphone (107): a funnel-shaped device used to project a voice

reputation (108): general esteem that one has from others

untarnished (109): once disgraced, but now that disgrace is taken away

Chapter 13

1. Why did Louis ask Sam to slit the web on his right foot? (Louis wanted to wiggle his toes and use the trumpet valves.)
2. Louis said that he had to have all of his possessions. Do you agree? Why or why not?
3. Which one do you think he needed the most?
4. What is your favorite possession?

valves (111): devices on an instrument used to vary the sound

hesitated (113): paused

tendency (114): inclination to act a certain way

plumage (116): the feathers of a bird

acquired (116): to get or have new skills

Chapter 14

1. What was Louis's new job? (Louis played for a swan boat in Boston.)
2. What advice do you have for the boatman?
3. If you were on the boat, what would you think of Louis?
4. Why couldn't Louis spend the night on the lake? (It was dangerous and Louis was a celebrity.)
5. What do you like and dislike about the boatman?

residents (118): people living in a place for a time

quadruple (122): multiplied by four

quintuple (122): multiplied by five

musician (124): person who plays music

Chapter 15

1. Why didn't the clerk at the Ritz Hotel want to give Louis a room? (Louis was a bird, he might have lice, and he might mess in the room.)
2. Would you let Louis stay at your house? Why or why not?
3. What were Louis's goals? (Louis wanted to restore his father's honor, pay for the trumpet, and take Serena for his wife.)
4. What is one of your goals?
5. Pretend that you are Sam. After reading the letter on page 136, write a response to Louis at the hotel.

sensation (126): a certain feeling

commotion (126): violent motion, disturbance

immaculate (127): perfectly clean

celebrity (127): famous person

summoned (129): called together

Chapter 16

1. The man in charge of the birds at the Philadelphia Zoo made an arrangement with Mr. Lucas concerning Louis. What was the arrangement? (Louis would not get pinioned, and he would be able to live at the zoo.)

2. What was Louis to do for the zoo in return for the favor? (Louis played his trumpet on Sundays.)

3. Do you think it was a fair trade? Why or why not?

echoed (141): repeated sounds over a distance

shrewd (143): clever, practical

moola (145): money

pinion (145): cut a section of a bird's wing to keep it from flying

candor (145): fairness

Chapter 17

1. What did Louis think of his new job? (Louis didn't like staying up late, but he did enjoy entertaining others.)

2. Describe Serena's arrival at Bird Lake. (She came down in a storm and almost died.)

3. What was Louis's plan to win Serena? (He planned to play a song for her when she woke up.)

4. How did Serena react to Louis? (The song filled her with joy and love.)

5. What do you like best about Louis?

employer (148): a person who hires someone else to do a job

exhausted (153): extremely tired

preening her feathers (153): combing her feathers

astonishment (160): amazement

solemnly (160): seriously

Chapter 18

1. What did Louis do to save Serena from being pinioned? (Louis beat up the zookeepers, and he wrote to Sam.)

2. What was Sam's idea to help save Serena? (They would donate a cygnet to the zoo each year.)

3. Do you think Louis will want to donate a cygnet to the zoo in years to come? Why or why not?

4. How did Sam show his friendship to Louis?

ornamental (164): decorative, adding beauty

valuable (169): having great worth

astounded (171): astonished, surprised

captive (172): held under control against one's will

persuade (172): convince

security (173): freedom from risk or danger

Chapter 19

1. What two things did Sam's trip to the zoo accomplish? (Sam saved Serena, and he decided what he wanted to be when he grows up.)
2. How much money did Louis have? (Louis had $4,691.65.)
3. Why are animals lucky?
4. Describe the trip from Philadelphia to Upper Red Rock Lake.

proposal (175): plan

fascinated (175): grabbed the interest of

profit (179): money earned after expenses have been subtracted

triumphant (184): victorious

penniless (184): poor

Chapter 20

1. Describe the commotion caused by the cob's arrival at the music store in Billings. (The owner of the store shot the cob.)
2. Describe the cob's wound. (It was superficial, only on the surface.)
3. Do you agree or disagree with the judge's decision on page 196? Explain your answer.
4. How did the storekeeper prove that he was an honorable man? (He gave the extra money to the Audubon Society.)

sincere (185): honest, genuine

inconvenience (186): put to trouble, annoying

redeem (186): to get or win back

complicated (192): difficult to understand or explain

superficial (195): on the surface

Chapter 21

1. Sam told his mom that Louis couldn't send any more letters. Why not? (He couldn't buy stamps.)
2. If Louis could write a letter to Sam, what would it say?
3. What adventure do you think Louis will remember the most? Why?

Reaching Out Through Reading Journal Reflections

The Trumpet of the Swan

Chapters 1–3

1. Why was Sam reluctant to tell his father about his discovery?
2. Tell about one thing you discovered by reading this chapter.
3. Why was the nesting place perfect?
4. Describe your favorite place.
5. Why did the female swan feel uneasy as she sat on her nest?
6. How did Sam save the day for the swan?
7. Describe the cob.

Chapters 4–5

1. Describe how the cob felt about fatherhood.
2. What makes you feel proud?
3. What are some of the dangers of the pond according to the cob?
4. What dangers do children face today?
5. How did the fifth cygnet greet Sam?
6. Why do you think the fifth cygnet greeted Sam that way?
7. What was different about Louis?
8. Why did this difference concern his mother?
9. The cob told Louis there may be some slight advantage in not being able to say anything. What was that advantage?
10. If you were one of Louis's brothers or sisters, what would you say to try to help him?

Chapters 6–7

1. How would the cygnets use their knowledge of flying?
2. What are the three parts of flying?
3. What would it be like to fly like a swan?
4. What do you think about Louis's decision to learn to read and write?

From *Reaching Out Through Reading*. © 1998 Carrie Sorby Duits and Adelle K. Dorman. Teacher Ideas Press. (800) 237-6124.

5. The game warden complimented Sam and his father. What is one compliment someone has given to you?

6. What did Mrs. Hammerbotham think of having Louis in class?

7. How would you feel about having a swan in class?

8. How would you help Louis?

Chapters 8–9

1. What feelings did Louis and his family have when Louis returned to Red Rock Lake?

2. How did Louis's love for Serena present a problem for Louis?

3. How would you feel if you couldn't communicate with your family?

4. What do you think Louis should do next?

5. What was the cob's idea to help Louis?

6. How do you think the cob will get the trumpet for Louis?

7. How did the cob get the trumpet? How did he feel afterward?

8. What did the cob sacrifice to get the trumpet?

9. Have you ever sacrificed something for someone else? Explain your answer.

10. Write a newspaper headline and article about the incident.

Chapters 10–11

1. How did Sam help Louis?

2. If you have gone to summer camp, describe how you felt when you were packing to go. If you have never been to camp, how do you think you would feel?

3. If you were going to camp tomorrow, what are the five most important things you would take with you?

4. How did the boys at Camp Kookooskoos receive Louis?

5. How do you feel about Applegate?

6. According to Mr. Brickle, why was the camp called Kookooskoos?

7. What do you think would be a good name for a camp?

8. What does respect mean to you?

Chapters 12–13

1. Why were the boys teasing Applegate, and what was the result?
2. How did Louis become the most distinguished counselor at camp?
3. How do you think Louis felt when Applegate said he still didn't like birds?
4. What do you wish you could tell Applegate? What do you wish you could tell Louis?
5. What do you think Louis will wear around his neck next?
6. Why did Louis ask Sam to slit the web on his right foot?
7. Louis said that he had to have all of his possessions. Do you agree? Why or why not?
8. Which one do you think he needed the most?
9. What is your favorite possession?

Chapters 14–15

1. What was Louis's new job?
2. What advice do you have for the boatman?
3. If you were on the boat, what would you think of Louis?
4. Why couldn't Louis spend the night on the lake?
5. What do you like and dislike about the boatman?
6. Why didn't the clerk at the Ritz Hotel want to give Louis a room?
7. Would you let Louis stay at your house? Why or why not?
8. What were Louis's goals?
9. What is one of your goals?
10. Pretend that you are Sam. After reading the letter on page 136, write a response to Louis at the hotel.

Chapters 16–17

1. The man in charge of the birds at the Philadelphia Zoo made an arrangement with Mr. Lucas concerning Louis. What was the arrangement?
2. What was Louis to do for the zoo in return for the favor?
3. Do you think it was a fair trade? Why or why not?
4. What did Louis think of his new job?

5. Describe Serena's arrival at Bird Lake.

6. What was Louis's plan to win Serena?

7. How did Serena react to Louis?

8. What do you like best about Louis?

Chapters 18–19

1. What did Louis do to save Serena from being pinioned?

2. What was Sam's idea to help save Serena?

3. Do you think Louis will want to donate a cygnet to the zoo in years to come? Why or why not?

4. How did Sam show his friendship to Louis?

5. What two things did Sam's trip to the zoo accomplish?

6. How much money did Louis have?

7. Why are animals lucky?

8. Describe the trip from Philadelphia to Upper Red Rock Lake.

Chapters 20–21

1. Describe the commotion caused by the cob's arrival at the music store in Billings.

2. Describe the cob's wound.

3. Do you agree or disagree with the judge's decision on page 196? Explain your answer.

4. How did the storekeeper prove that he was an honorable man?

5. Sam told his mom that Louis couldn't send any more letters. Why not?

6. If Louis could write a letter to Sam, what would it say?

7. What adventure do you think Louis will remember the most? Why?

From *Reaching Out Through Reading.* © 1998 Carrie Sorby Duits and Adelle K. Dorman. Teacher Ideas Press. (800) 237-6124.

The Trumpet of the Swan

Name _____

by E. B. White

Sam Beaver wrote in his diary every night. Pretend you are Louis. Pick an event from your life as a celebrity swan and write a diary entry. Discuss the situation and the way you feel about it. End the diary entry with a question.

Dear Diary . . .

Louis

Dragonwings

Laurence Yep. New York: HarperTrophy, 1975. 248 pages.
Intermediate grade levels.

Dragonwings is historical fiction about Moon Shadow, a young Chinese boy who recently immigrated to the United States to join his father. Together, they work to pursue Father's dream to build a flying machine. Along the way, they encounter many hardships, but also build a special bond of love.

Dragonwings is an especially good text because it provides the unique viewpoint of a newly arrived Chinese immigrant. Thus, the book provides important insights to classrooms interested in multicultural learning. In addition, *Dragonwings* is true to history in many respects. Examples of the real events in *Dragonwings* include a San Francisco earthquake, restrictions on allowing Chinese wives into the country, and the flight of one of the first aeroplanes by a Chinese immigrant.

Some important messages to gain from this book are:

❖ It is important to follow your dreams.

❖ It is important to remember your own history.

❖ A person's skin color can't tell you what they are like inside.

❖ Discrimination is hurtful.

❖ Moving to a new country can be frightening and confusing.

❖ Doing drugs can hurt you and those around you.

❖ When people work together, great things can be accomplished.

ACTIVITY BRIDGE TO SERVICE LEARNING

Have students draw a picture of themselves doing an activity that is fun. Allow students to share their pictures. Discuss why all of the pictures are not of the same activity.

Give each student a copy of the *Dragonwings* worksheet (page 145) to complete.

After students have compared dragons, follow up with a discussion. This activity is meant to increase student awareness of different viewpoints. This can be helpful in leading to a service learning project because it asks students to consider others' opinions. Ask students: How might the recipient of your service react? What can you do to be especially considerate of their wishes and viewpoints?

Suggested Service Learning Projects

Raise money for a homeless shelter.

Adopt a family that is new to our country.

Invite guest speakers to talk to the class about preventing drug abuse.

Related Literature

McKissack, Pat, and Frederick McKissack. *Taking a Stand Against Racism and Racial Discrimination*. New York: Franklin Watts, 1990.

Muse, Daphne, ed. *Prejudice: Stories About Hate, Ignorance, Revelation, and Transformation*. New York: Hyperion, 1995.

Wilkinson, Brenda Scott. *Not Separate, Not Equal*. New York: Harper & Row, 1987.

Discussion Questions and Vocabulary

Chapter 1

1. What do the kites mean to Moon Shadow? (They are links to his father.)

2. What do you think Moon Shadow is feeling now that he will be joining his father on the Land of the Golden Mountain? (Apprehension, worry, excitement.)

lynched (1): hanged by a mob

debts (3): money that you owe

invest (3): to give money for the purpose of obtaining profit

dynasty (3): a series of rulers who are members of the same family

dictation (3): when someone writes down what you're saying

Chapter 2

1. When Father gave Moon Shadow the butterfly kite, what do you think it meant to Moon Shadow? (It was a special and significant gift. It was as if Father gave Moon Shadow a piece of himself.)

flatiron (15): an old iron, heated on a stove

rigorously (16): severely

scrolls (19): rolls of paper used for writing

Boxer Rebellion (25): an unsuccessful Chinese rebellion against outsiders

socialist (25): someone who believes in collective or government ownership of business, rather than individual ownership of business

provincial (25): belonging to a certain territory

raiment (27): clothing

queue (27): a ponytail

brooding (28): thinking deeply, usually unhappily

opium (29): an intoxicating drug that is smoked

insolent (29): disrespectful

Chapter 3

1. How do you think you would feel after your first day in a new country?

2. The Dragon King told Windrider, "You must prove yourself worthy to be a dragon once more, and you can only do that by passing a series of tests." What sort of tests do you think the Dragon King meant?

3. When Uncle gave Moon Shadow the monkey, why do you think he wanted Moon Shadow to keep secret who had given it to him? (Uncle didn't want his tough image to be changed with the rest of the Company.)

filaments (33): fine metal wires, like those in a lightbulb

defiance (43): resistance to authority

aerial (43): in the air

rheumatic (47): having pain in the joints and muscles

Chapter 4

1. Why did Moon Shadow's grandfather die? (He died to defend his honor.) Was his death worth his pride?

2. Windrider refused to take a tip from Mr. Alger. Why? (He was happy to have the chance to work on a car.) What was Mr. Alger's reaction? (He was surprised and pleased at Windrider's integrity. He told Windrider that he would hire him if he ever needed work.)

3. Why did Uncle refuse to believe that the Wright brothers' aeroplane had flown? (He thought it was foolish for people to fly.) Once he accepted it, why did he continue to act as if he were upset? (He wanted to discourage Windrider.)

obligations (52): promises or duties

revolutionary (53): a person who fights the existing government

intuitive (56): able to know without conscious thought

diagram (58): a sketch, plan, or graph

surly (59): bad-tempered

loftily (62): in an overly proud manner

proclamations (63): announcements

dirigibles (63): early blimps

grudged (67): admitted without wanting to

confrontation (68): conflict

chided (68): scolded, teased

Chapter 5

1. Why does Black Dog think that America is ugly? (Because of the racism and the trouble with drugs he has encountered.)

2. Why did Father hit Lefty? (He had to get him out of the way.)

3. Moon Shadow and his father will now live among the demons. What sorts of dangers do they face? (They face violence, prejudice, poverty, being farther away from the support of the Company.)

abacus (76): a manual calculator developed by the Chinese

simpering (81): silly, self-conscious

compensation (92): payment given to make up for something

incense (93): a material that is burned to make a pleasant smell

Chapter 6

1. What does Miss Whitlaw's dragon look like? (Evil, bad.)

2. What does Moon Shadow's dragon look like? (Strong, good.)

3. Draw a picture of both dragons, showing their differences and similarities.

dray horses (96): horses that haul low, heavy carts

brood (96): a family group

dubiously (103): uncertainly

malicious (111): mean

Chapter 7

1. What kind of a woman is Miss Whitlaw? (She is giving and kind.) Why does Moon Shadow think that he must have known her in another life? (He thinks that she is too kind to be a demoness.)

2. Does Moon Shadow's experience with the demon boys put him in serious danger? Why? (It might put him in danger because they know where he lives.)

3. Why did Robin volunteer to help Moon Shadow learn to read? (She is his friend and wants to help him.)

4. Have you ever volunteered to help another person? How did it make you feel?

tentatively (116): uncertainly

tenement (118): an inexpensive apartment in very poor condition

ambushed (120): attacked by surprise

erratically (124): unpredictably

mused (124): pondered, considered

jargon (124): specialized words used in certain situations or by certain people, for example doctors use medical jargon

configuration (124): shape

skeptical (125): doubtful

province (126): territory

mulled (126): thought seriously about

Chapter 8

1. How did Moon Shadow feel about Robin at the beginning of the chapter? (He enjoys her company, and he feels proud to be able to teach her some things about flying.)

2. How did Moon Shadow feel about Robin when Father lets her fly the glider? (He is jealous because Father let her fly it first.)

3. How does Moon Shadow feel about Robin at the end of the chapter? (He has gotten over his jealousy.)

4. Discuss what Miss Whitlaw meant when she said, "We see the same thing and yet find different truths" (p. 147). In what, besides constellations, do they find different truths? (Religion, myths.)

correspondence (134): communication through letters

indecisively (138): without decision

exhilarating (138): exciting

patronized (142): talked down to

constellations (146): groups of stars

Chapter 9

1. Father called Miss Whitlaw a "superior woman." What are some of the ways that Miss Whitlaw has proven herself to be a superior woman? (By helping others in the earthquake and by being a good friend to Moon Shadow and Windrider.)

somber (150): serious

boycott (151): refusing to buy products for a reason

choler (153): the characteristic of being easily angered

querulous (157): fretful

moral persuasion (160): convincing someone to believe in acting a certain way

shanghaier (161): kidnapper

martial law (168): temporary rule by the military in times of trouble

salvaging (168): saving

Chapter 10

1. Uncle said, "Superior men help one another in time of need" (p. 178). Write at least two times when members of the Company helped each other in time of need. (Bringing Moon Shadow to America, bringing Black Dog home.)

2. Why would Robin and Miss Whitlaw be afraid of being guests of the Company? (They were still very unfamiliar with Tang people and customs.)

3. Why does Uncle like Miss Whitlaw? (She brought brandy, she tried to eat with chopsticks, she could talk about the railroad.)

4. Why don't the demons want the Tang to move back to Tang people's town? (They want to build demon buildings on the land.)

5. How do the Tang plan to return to their town? Why is the plan a good one? (They will refuse to provide service to the demons; they will move to another city. This is a good plan because so much of the demon's way of life is dependent on the Tang people's service.)

6. Is it right for Father to pursue his dream? Why or why not?

ineptitude (185): being unable

deities (185): gods

malicious (188): mean and spiteful

incredulously (188): doubtfully, unable to believe

haughty (188): lofty

contemptuously (191): scornfully

sardonically (195): sarcastically, bitterly

indifferent (197): without care

impulsively (198): without thinking

defiantly (198): rebelliously

scandalized (199): outraged

Chapter 11

1. What did Moon Shadow mean when he said, "There was some beauty to life after all, even if it was only the beauty of hope" (p. 224)? (Black Dog has lost the beauty of hope, but Moon Shadow and Windrider still have it.) Whom do you know who holds the beauty of hope?

revelations (205): important realizations

ambition (215): goal

undernourished (217): very underfed

plucky (218): high-spirited

Chapter 12

1. When you read about Father wanting to fly, what did you think he might have been thinking? How was it different from what he said he was thinking about on pages 241–242? (He had to go through the test, but now that it's over he feels like he has to concentrate on his family.)

2. Have you ever felt like Moon Shadow felt when he said: "And all of a sudden I saw that if life seems awfully petty most of the time, every now and then there is something noble and beautiful and almost pure that lifts us suddenly out of the pettiness and lets us share in it a little" (p. 233)? What made you feel that way?

abominable (226): loathsome

penance (227): acts that are done to make up for wrongdoing

compensation (229): payment or repayment

convert (230): to change

dubiously (230): doubtfully

ingratiatingly (232): with flattery

petty (233): little, trivial, insignificant

auspicious (234): outstanding or significant

cordial (235): an alcoholic drink

exhilarated (236): thrilled

Afterword

1. Compare what happens in *Dragonwings* to what was really going on during the early 1900s. Use reference materials to make the comparisons. (An earthquake in San Francisco, Tang women not being allowed into America, racism, a Tang man flying, the Wright brothers.)

ingenious (247): creative, brilliant

stereotypes (248): generalizations about a group of people

Reaching Out Through Reading Journal Reflections

Dragonwings

Chapters 1–3

1. What do the kites mean to Moon Shadow?

2. What do you think Moon Shadow is feeling now that he will be joining his father on the Land of the Golden Mountain?

3. When Father gave Moon Shadow the butterfly kite, what do you think it meant to Moon Shadow?

4. How do you think you would feel after your first day in a new country?

5. The Dragon King told Windrider, "You must prove yourself worthy to be a dragon once more, and you can only do that by passing a series of tests." What sort of tests do you think the Dragon King meant?

6. When Uncle gave Moon Shadow the monkey, why do you think he wanted Moon Shadow to keep secret who had given it to him?

Chapters 4–5

1. Why did Moon Shadow's grandfather die? Was his death worth his pride?

2. Windrider refused to take a tip from Mr. Alger. Why? What was Mr. Alger's reaction?

3. Why did Uncle refuse to believe that the Wright brothers' aeroplane had flown? Once he accepted it, why did he continue to act as if he were upset?

4. Why does Black Dog think that America is ugly?

5. Why did Father hit Lefty?

6. Moon Shadow and his father will now live among the demons. What sorts of dangers do they face?

Chapters 6–7

1. What does Miss Whitlaw's dragon look like?
2. What does Moon Shadow's dragon look like?
3. Draw a picture of both dragons, showing their differences and similarities.
4. What kind of a woman is Miss Whitlaw? Why does Moon Shadow think that he must have known her in another life?
5. Does Moon Shadow's experience with the demon boys put him in serious danger? Why?
6. Why did Robin volunteer to help Moon Shadow learn to read?
7. Have you ever volunteered to help another person? How did it make you feel?

Chapters 8–9

1. How did Moon Shadow feel about Robin at the beginning of the chapter?
2. How did Moon Shadow feel about Robin when Father lets her fly the glider?
3. How does Moon Shadow feel about Robin at the end of the chapter?
4. Discuss what Miss Whitlaw meant when she said, "We see the same thing and yet find different truths" (p. 147). In what, besides constellations, do they find different truths?
5. Father called Miss Whitlaw a "superior woman." What are some of the ways that Miss Whitlaw has proven herself to be a superior woman?

Chapters 10–11

1. Uncle said, "Superior men help one another in time of need" (p. 178). Write at least two times when members of the Company helped each other in time of need.
2. Why would Robin and Miss Whitlaw be afraid of being guests of the Company?
3. Why does Uncle like Miss Whitlaw?
4. Why don't the demons want the Tang to move back to Tang people's town?
5. How do the Tang plan to return to their town? Why is the plan a good one?
6. Is it right for Father to pursue his dream? Why or why not?
7. What did Moon Shadow mean when he said, "There was some beauty to life after all, even if it was only the beauty of hope" (p. 224)? Whom do you know who holds the beauty of hope?

Chapters 12–Afterword

1. When you read about Father wanting to fly, what did you think he might have been thinking? How was it different from what he said he was thinking about on pages 241–242?

2. Have you ever felt like Moon Shadow felt when he said: "And all of a sudden I saw that if life seems awfully petty most of the time, every now and then there is something noble and beautiful and almost pure that lifts us suddenly out of the pettiness and lets us share in it a little" (p. 233)? What made you feel that way?

3. Compare what happens in *Dragonwings* to what was really going on during the early 1900s.

Dragonwings
by Laurence Yep

Name _____

In the squares below, draw what Moon Shadow's dragon looks like. Draw what Miss Whitlaw's dragon looks like. In the space beside the pictures, write *why* Moon Shadow's and Miss Whitlaw's dragons are different. (Do not explain *what* makes them different, but *why* they are different.)

Moon Shadow's Dragon

Miss Whitlaw's Dragon

From the Mixed-Up Files of Mrs. Basil E. Frankweiler

E. L. Konigsburg. New York: Dell, 1987. 159 pages.
Intermediate grade levels.

Tired of the injustices of living at home, Claudia schemes to run away to the New York Metropolitan Museum of Art. She talks her brother, Jamie, into the adventure because he has saved some money. While hiding at the museum, Claudia and Jamie learn that the origin of a beautiful angel statue in the museum is a mystery to museum officials. The angel may be the work of Michelangelo.

Only one person knows what artist created the statue. Her name is Mrs. Basil E. Frankweiler. In an effort to become "different," the children investigate the mystery. They finally decide to visit Mrs. Basil E. Frankweiler to learn the truth about the statue. But the answer is not that simple. They are given one hour to research in her mixed-up files. The truth about the artist who created the angel is exchanged for the details of their story as runaway children.

Some important messages to gain from this book are:

❖ Take time to reflect upon your learning.

❖ Learn about yourself and discover your own special qualities.

❖ Appreciate learning.

❖ Appreciate art.

Activity Bridge to Service Learning

Share several prints of works by Renaissance artists. (Or share books about the artists and their work.) Possibilities include da Vinci, El Greco, and Raphael.

Ask students to compare and contrast the works of art. How are they alike? How are they different? Record students' responses.

Give each student a copy of the *From the Mixed-Up Files of Mrs. Basil E. Frankweiler* worksheet (page 155) to complete.

Follow up with a discussion. Claudia and Mrs. Frankweiler both wanted to make meaningful contributions. What did they give to each other? What did we learn from Claudia and Mrs. Frankweiler? Use the Three-Column Brainstorming tool (part 3) to complete the discussion.

SUGGESTED SERVICE LEARNING PROJECTS

Raise money to contribute to a home for runaway children.

Set up a buddy system with a younger class so students can share what they have learned each week.

Adopt an elderly man or woman as a classroom grandparent.

Raise money to buy Renaissance art prints for the school. Have groups of students study various artists and share their discoveries with other students.

Contribute funds to the local art museum.

Send "Angel Grams" (notes and letters) to patients in a nursing home.

RELATED LITERATURE

Avi. *Beyond the Western Sea*. New York: Orchard Books, 1996.

Fischetto, Laura. *Michael the Angel*. New York: Doubleday, 1993.

Kiser, SuAnn. *The Catspring Somersault Flying One-Handed Flip-Flop*. New York: Orchard Books, 1993.

Kraus, Robert. *Where Are You Going, Little Mouse?* New York: Greenwillow Books, 1986.

Lace, William W. *Michelangelo*. San Diego: Lucent Books, 1993.

Radley, Gail. *The Golden Days*. New York: Macmillan, 1991.

Richmond, Robin. *Introducing Michelangelo*. Boston: Little, Brown, 1992.

Sachs, Marilyn. *At the Sound of the Beep*. New York: Dutton Children's Books, 1990.

Strommen, Judith Bernie. *Grady the Great*. New York: Alfred A. Knopf, 1993.

Venezia, Mike. *Michelangelo*. Chicago: Children's Press, 1991.

DISCUSSION QUESTIONS AND VOCABULARY

Chapter 1

1. Why does Claudia want to run away? Give at least three reasons. (She feels injustice. She had to set the table and empty the dishwasher on the same night. Every week is the same. She is bored and tired of monotony.)

2. What injustices do you face?

3. Claudia lost her allowance because she broke household rules. If you could make up the rules for your house, what would they be?

4. Are you more like Claudia or Jamie? Explain your answer.

5. What do you think will be the details of Claudia's plan?

companion (11): a friend to travel with

injustice (12): a wrong, something that is not fair

despised (15): hated

impatient (19): not willing to wait, eager

complications (20): complex difficulties

Chapter 2

1. What would you pack in a violin case?

2. What do you think about Claudia's plan?

3. How do you think her parents will react to Claudia's note?

wholeheartedly (24): sincerely, holding nothing back

expenditures (31): amounts of money that are spent

Chapter 3

1. Why will it be important for Jamie to be a cheapskate? (They will not have an income. They don't have a lot of money, so everything seems expensive.)

2. Describe their hiding place. (The museum is huge, with visitors from around the world, and admission is free. Their hiding place is an elegant room with fine French and English furniture.)

3. What complications do you think they will run into?

4. The book says that Claudia and Jamie became a team and that this involved special feelings. Describe a time when you felt a part of a team. How did you feel?

5. Why do you think Claudia and Jamie felt so tired at the end of the day?

extravagant (33): exceeding reasonable limits

cheapskate (34): one who does not like to spend large amounts of money

inconspicuous (35): not easily noticed

destination (38): the place where one is headed

veto power (38): the power to reject a vote

fussbudget (43): a person who fusses over little things

Chapter 4

1. Where did Claudia and Jamie hide their personal belongings in the museum? (In a sarcophagus, behind a tapestry screen, in a huge urn, and tucked behind a drape.)

2. Where would you hide your belongings?

3. What wonderful opportunity did Claudia believe they had while hiding in the museum? (The opportunity to learn and study.)

4. What important lessons have you learned outside the classroom? Describe what you did and how you felt as a learner.

5. What is the most important thing you have learned about Mrs. Frankweiler?

sarcophagus (48): a stone coffin

convenience (48): something to make one more comfortable

commotion (56): noisy confusion

impostor (58): one who assumes a false identity

acquisition (62): something that one becomes the owner of

curators (62): the people in charge of a museum

Chapter 5

1. How did Claudia and Jamie plan to study Angel? (They went to the library. Claudia read and Jamie looked at the pictures.)
2. How is their life at the museum much like their life at home? (Baths, bedtime, schooling.)
3. How is their life different at the museum?
4. Claudia believes that you can learn a lot about a person when you hug them. What do you think you can learn?
5. Why do you think Claudia and Jamie aren't homesick?
6. Describe a time when you were homesick.

persuade (70): convince

determination (72): having a definite decision

irritable (76): easily annoyed

humility (76): the state of being meek and humble

conscience (87): ability and urge to distinguish right from wrong

Chapter 6

1. What important clue did Jamie and Claudia discover? (The three rings in the carpet.)
2. Why did Claudia want to know the truth about Angel before she went home?
3. Describe a time when you felt special and different.
4. How do you think the museum officials will respond to the letter? What will they write in return?

stonemason's mark (97): the signature mark of a person who works with stone

feeling triumphant (97): feeling victorious, feeling like a winner

disguise (100): to hide one's identity

Chapter 7

1. What surprise did Claudia and Jamie have when they looked for someone to deliver the letter? (Jamie's class was touring the museum.)
2. How did they use this discovery to their advantage? (They used the school name to identify themselves when delivering the letter.)
3. Jamie made up a name for himself, Angelo Michaels from Marblehead, Massachusetts.
4. Make up another name for Claudia.

5. How are Jamie and Claudia a terrific team?

stowaways (106): people who secretly board a vehicle

familiarity (106): knowing something or someone very well

Chapter 8

1. How do Claudia and Jamie feel about each other? How do you know?
2. Why do you think Claudia wants to be different?
3. Summarize the letter from the museum.
4. Why did Claudia cry?
5. What would you have told Claudia to encourage her?
6. Why was Claudia comforted as she remembered Mrs. Basil E. Frankweiler?

casually (111): showing little concern

quarried (114): taken from an open pit

evidence (115): something that provides proof

consensus (115): reaching agreement

self-assurance (122): sure of oneself

Chapter 9

1. How do you think Claudia feels about Mrs. Basil E. Frankweiler? Why?
2. Why was Mrs. Frankweiler's office a surprise to the children? (It looks more like a laboratory. There is nothing fancy about it. It is lined with rows and rows of filing cabinets.)
3. How did Mrs. Basil E. Frankweiler prove to be a smart lady?
4. What important matter does Mrs. Basil E. Frankweiler share with the children? (Their parents are frantic about their missing children.)
5. How did Claudia's habit of planning prove to be important? (They made a list of what files to look in so they could make good use of their time.)
6. Plan a family reunion party for Claudia and Jamie. Start with a list, as Claudia and Jamie did.
7. Why doesn't Mrs. Basil E. Frankweiler tell the museum about Angel? (They would doubt everything, send in experts, and destroy the beauty and mystery of the Angel.)
8. How are Mrs. Basil E. Frankweiler and Claudia alike?
9. What does Mrs. Basil E. Frankweiler teach us all about learning new things? (We need to have days when we don't learn new things. Instead, we need to take time and let all that we know swell up inside us. Otherwise, we just fill ourselves with facts that rattle around inside us.)

10. How do you feel about Mrs. Basil E. Frankweiler? Why?

paupers (124): poor people

intrigued (125): curious

astounded (135): overwhelmed with amazement

charity (136): a gift to the public

sympathy (138): sharing common feelings

sauntered (143): walked leisurely, strolled

Chapter 10

1. Why do you think Mrs. Basil E. Frankweiler sold Angel to the museum?

2. Who is Saxonberg? (Mrs. Basil E. Frankweiler's lawyer and the children's grandfather.)

3. How will the children make Mrs. Basil E. Frankweiler their grandmother?

4. What suggestions do you have for them?

5. List the main characters in the book and the secrets they keep.

6. What finally happened to Angel? (The drawing is bequeathed to the children and they will keep the secret. The museum will continue to investigate the mystery.)

preoccupied (152): lost in thought

accurate (153): free from error

bequeathing (157): giving something to another person, often through a will

Reaching Out Through Reading Journal Reflections

From the Mixed-Up Files of Mrs. Basil E. Frankweiler

Chapters 1–2

1. Why does Claudia want to run away? Give at least three reasons.

2. What injustices do you face?

3. Claudia lost her allowance because she broke household rules. If you could make up the rules for your house, what would they be?

4. Are you more like Claudia or Jamie? Explain your answer.

5. What do you think will be the details of Claudia's plan?

6. What would you pack in a violin case?

7. What do you think about Claudia's plan?

8. How do you think her parents will react to Claudia's note?

Chapters 3–4

1. Why will it be important for Jamie to be a cheapskate?

2. Describe their hiding place.

3. What complications do you think they will run into?

4. The book says that Claudia and Jamie became a team and that this involved special feelings. Describe a time when you felt a part of a team. How did you feel?

5. Why do you think Claudia and Jamie felt so tired at the end of the day?

6. Where did Claudia and Jamie hide their personal belongings in the museum?

7. Where would you hide your belongings?

8. What wonderful opportunity did Claudia believe they had while hiding in the museum?

9. What important lessons have you learned outside the classroom? Describe what you did and how you felt as a learner.

10. What is the most important thing you have learned about Mrs. Frankweiler?

From *Reaching Out Through Reading*. © 1998 Carrie Sorby Duits and Adelle K. Dorman. Teacher Ideas Press. (800) 237-6124.

Chapters 5–6

1. How did Claudia and Jamie plan to study Angel?

2. How is their life at the museum much like their life at home?

3. How is their life different at the museum?

4. Claudia believes that you can learn a lot about a person when you hug them. What do you think you can learn?

5. Why do you think Claudia and Jamie aren't homesick?

6. Describe a time when you were homesick.

7. What important clue did Jamie and Claudia discover?

8. Why did Claudia want to know the truth about Angel before she went home?

9. Describe a time when you felt special and different.

10. How do you think the museum officials will respond to the letter? What will they write in return?

Chapters 7–8

1. What surprise did Claudia and Jamie have when they looked for someone to deliver the letter?

2. How did they use this discovery to their advantage?

3. Jamie made up a name for himself, Angelo Michaels from Marblehead, Massachusetts. Make up another name for Claudia.

4. How are Jamie and Claudia a terrific team?

5. How do Claudia and Jamie feel about each other? How do you know?

6. Why do you think Claudia wants to be different?

7. Summarize the letter from the museum.

8. Why did Claudia cry?

9. What would you have told Claudia to encourage her?

10. Why was Claudia comforted as she remembered Mrs. Basil E. Frankweiler?

Chapter 9

1. How do you think Claudia feels about Mrs. Basil E. Frankweiler? Why?
2. Why was Mrs. Frankweiler's office a surprise to the children?
3. How did Mrs. Basil E. Frankweiler prove to be a smart lady?
4. What important matter does Mrs. Basil E. Frankweiler share with the children?
5. How did Claudia's habit of planning prove to be important?
6. Plan a family reunion party for Claudia and Jamie. Start with a list, as Claudia and Jamie did.
7. Why doesn't Mrs. Basil E. Frankweiler tell the museum about Angel?
8. How are Mrs. Basil E. Frankweiler and Claudia alike?
9. What does Mrs. Basil E. Frankweiler teach us all about learning new things?
10. How do you feel about Mrs. Basil E. Frankweiler? Why?

Chapter 10

1. Why do you think Mrs. Basil E. Frankweiler sold Angel to the museum?
2. Who is Saxonberg?
3. How will the children make Mrs. Basil E. Frankweiler their grandmother?
4. What suggestions do you have for them?
5. List the main characters in the book and the secrets they keep.
6. What finally happened to Angel?

From *Reaching Out Through Reading.* © 1998 Carrie Sorby Duits and Adelle K. Dorman. Teacher Ideas Press. (800) 237-6124.

From the Mixed-Up Files of Mrs. Basil E. Frankweiler

Name _____

by E. L. Konigsburg

How are Claudia and Mrs. Frankweiler alike? How are they different? Fill in the diagram below to compare these two characters.

Claudia

Mrs. Frankweiler and Claudia

Mrs. Frankweiler

Which character is most like you? How? Why?

_____

_____

Roll of Thunder, Hear My Cry

Mildred D. Taylor. New York: Bantam Books, 1976. 276 pages.
Intermediate grade levels.

This literature unit offers students important building blocks for exploring issues related to prejudice and for providing service to their communities. Mildred D. Taylor's *Roll of Thunder, Hear My Cry* is a Newbery Medal winner that promotes thought and discussion about democratic ideals. Challenging for the fifth-grade reading level, the novel powerfully depicts the struggle of an African American family in Mississippi during the post–Civil War era. It addresses issues such as prejudice, community building, racial violence, individual and group resistance to oppression, and the uneven distribution of wealth. The novel provides excellent opportunities to compare the experiences of the Logan family with the real-life experiences of people like Malcolm X, Martin Luther King Jr., and Harriet Tubman. The novel also highlights the importance of diversity and its benefits to the community.

In addition to the novel, other resources in various media may be used, such as the video *A Time for Justice*, the newspaper *Pride in Color*, the books *Autobiography of Malcolm X*, *The People Could Fly*, and *Hey Mom, Can I Ride My Bike Across America?* Jim Crow laws and landmark court cases, such as *Plessy* v. *Ferguson* and *Brown* v. *Board of Education*, may be discussed within this context.

Several classroom strategies are helpful in presenting this unit. Double-entry journals and symbolic analysis encourage students to delve deeply into the issues. Although readers theatre can be time-consuming, it is strongly recommended. (The box on page 157 contains instructions for conducting readers theatre for chapter 7.) Each piece added to the unit provides additional opportunities for students to express themselves and to learn in various ways. This, in turn, provides students with a rich bed of ideas from which to develop a service component for the unit.

Because this text is difficult to read, consider combining teacher and student read-alouds and silent reading.

Some important messages to gain from this book are:

❖ It is important to remember American history.

❖ Hatred is often based in ignorance.

❖ Working hard is important.

❖ In tough times it is important to stick together.

Chapter 7: Readers Theatre

Instead of reading chapter 7, assign students a section to read and act out with other students. This process takes about three days for preparation and presentation, but the delay allows students who are behind in their reading to catch up. It also gives students an opportunity to engage in a meaningful readers theatre.

Chapter 7 (prepared for 30 students)

Group Number	Page Numbers	Number of Students
1	106–109	3
2	109–110	2
3	110–114	5
4	114–116	4
5	116	2
6	116–119	4
7	119–120	2
8	120–125	4
9	125–129	4

ACTIVITY BRIDGE TO SERVICE LEARNING

Have students working in small groups give an example of "There are two sides to every story." Allow student groups to share their examples.

Give each student a copy of the *Roll of Thunder, Hear My Cry* worksheet (page 165) to complete.

This activity is an exercise to help students understand different viewpoints. This is an extremely valuable exercise before students provide service, as it increases awareness of how things are interpreted differently by different people. Students should discuss how they can be most sensitive to those they serve.

SUGGESTED SERVICE LEARNING PROJECTS

Support Habitat for Humanity: Help on a work site, raise money, or work to increase community awareness and participation in Habitat for Humanity projects.

Serve the sick: Send cheery cards to a hospital, make a banner for someone who is homebound, make a tape of songs and send it to someone who is sick.

Promote public safety: Learn about fire prevention and what to do in case of fire. Share the information with younger students by writing and giving a presentation or skit.

Build public awareness about prejudice: Invite some elderly people to talk to your class about prejudice they have encountered and whether attitudes have changed over time or from place to place. Share the information in a class bulletin, newsletter, or bulletin board display.

Related Literature

Boettner, John. *Hey Mom, Can I Ride My Bike Across America?* Brea, CA: Seigel Bottner Fulton, 1990.

Haley, Alex. *The Autobiography of Malcolm X*. New York: Ballantine Books, 1965.

Harris, Dorothea. *Pride in Color*. No publication information available.

McKissack, Pat, and Frederick McKissack. *Taking a Stand Against Racism and Racial Discrimination*. New York: Franklin Watts, 1990.

Muse, Daphne, ed. *Prejudice: Stories About Hate, Ignorance, Revelation, and Transformation*. New York: Hyperion, 1995.

Taylor, Mildred D. *The Friendship*. New York: Dial Books for Young Readers, 1987.

——. *The Gold Cadillac*. New York: Dial Books for Young Readers, 1987.

——. *Let the Circle Be Unbroken*. New York: Dial Press, 1981. (Sequel to *Roll of Thunder, Hear My Cry*).

——. *The Road to Memphis*. New York: Dial Books for Young Readers, 1990.

——. *Song of the Trees*. New York: Dial Press, 1975.

——. *The Well: David's Story*. New York: Dial Books for Young Readers, 1995.

Wilkinson, Brenda Scott. *Not Separate, Not Equal*. New York: Harper & Row, 1987.

Discussion Questions and Vocabulary

Chapter 1

1. In the first two chapters, what do you learn about Mississippi after the Civil War? (Racism is still rampant.)

2. What is unusual about the land that Cassie lives on? (Her family owns it.)

3. What is unusual about Jeremy? (He is friendly to Cassie and her family.)

4. Is Little Man giving himself "airs," as Miss Crocker claims on page 23? (He is not acting pretentious, he is only angry that the African American students receive the white students' leftovers.)

5. Analyze the stamp found in Little Man's book on page 25. What would you have thought about or done if you were Little Man?

6. Was it right for Miss Crocker to switch Little Man and Cassie? What would you have done if you were Miss Crocker?

7. How did Cassie know her Mama understands about the books? (Cassie saw Mama gluing covers on her own students' books.)

sharecropping (3): working on someone else's land for a share of the crops

disdainfully (7): to look down on someone or something in a way that shows they are considered inferior

temerity (16): foolish boldness

chignon (20): a knot or coil of hair worn at the base of the neck

maverick (22): a person who acts independently and has personal ideas about how things should be

imperiously (22): to do something in a way that is overbearing and arrogant

ginned (24): how cotton is separated from the seeds

tawny (24): brownish-yellow; tan

chiffonier (26): chest of drawers

Chapter 2

1. Why is the book titled *Roll of Thunder, Hear My Cry*? (Mr. Morrison has come to help. His voice is like a roll of thunder.)

2. What do you think Mama meant when she told Mr. Morrison, "You're lucky no worse happened and we're glad to have you here . . . especially now"? (Mama feels that with the additional racial tension, it will be good to have Mr. Morrison around the farm.)

moronic (36): crazy

conspiratorially (37): acting as if secretly plotting

maneuvered (41): planned

Chapter 3

1. Using a dictionary to help you, define racism.

2. What are some examples of racism in this book?

caravan (53): group of cars

feigned (56): pretended

Chapter 4

1. Stacey knew he could get into serious trouble if he fought with T. J., but he did it anyway. Was it worth it? Why?

2. What makes the land important to Big Ma? (She has history on the land. She takes pride in owning it.)

3. What problems will the families face if they decide to shop in Vicksburg? List the problems discussed in chapter 4, and think about other problems they may face. (Violence is the greatest concern; another problem is losing credit at local stores.)

mercantile (81): a huge shopping center with many farmers selling goods

malevolently (84): in a manner that wishes evil or harm to others

Chapter 5

1. The Civil War has been over for some time. Why does Big Ma still have to park her wagon far away from the white parking areas? (Slavery is over, but segregation remains.)

2. Why do you think Cassie asked to be served after waiting so long? (She didn't think it was right to have to wait for white orders to be filled.)

3. Respond to the following quote from Mr. Barnett: " 'Get her out of here,' he said with hateful force, 'And make sure she don't come back till yo' mammy teach her what she is' " (p. 112).

4. Why did Big Ma make Cassie apologize to Lillian Jean? Why was it the right thing to do? Why was it the wrong thing to do? (It was the right thing to do because it avoided a lot of trouble. Apologizing was the wrong thing to do because it wasn't Cassie's fault.)

interminable (109): seeming to last forever

consoling (109): comforting or cheering up someone

shantytown (112): a place with small, shabby homes

avenging (113): getting revenge

mulatto (116): a person with one African American parent and one white parent

Chapter 6

1. In your own words, explain what Mama told Cassie about why white people think they are better than African Americans. (Hint: Look on pages 126–130.)

2. What would you like to tell Cassie?

credit (115): getting something, like groceries, and paying for them later, often with interest

aristocracy (121): a government ruled by a privileged, wealthy upper class

collateral (122): something of value, like land, promised to your creditor if you can't pay what you owe

eviction (123): to be forced to leave your home if you can't pay the mortgage or rent

boycott (124): to refuse to buy, sell, or use something for a reason

insolently (127): disrespectfully

Yankee carpetbaggers (128): Northerners who come to the South to take advantage of the unsettled conditions after the Civil War

Uncle Tomming (132): acting white to fit in or get special attention or favors from whites

sentinels (133): people guarding a group against surprise or attack

indignant (138): feeling or expressing anger or scorn, especially at mean or unjust action

Chapter 7

1. Why does Cassie believe Papa when he tells her they will never lose their land? (Because Papa is trying to believe it himself.)

2. Why does Mr. Granger come to visit? (To try to scare them.)

morosely (143): acting gloomy and sad

despondently (169): without courage, confidence, or hope

condemning (170): strongly disapproving

Chapter 8

1. Discuss two main reasons Mama was fired. (She was teaching true history instead of "white" history; she was trying to get families to shop in Vicksburg; she "destroyed" school property.)

2. Respond to a passage of your choice from chapter 8.

condescending (182): looking down upon

resigned (185): gave up

wary (186): cautious

despicable (189): detestable

akimbo (191): with hands on hips and elbows bent

affirmation (194): agreement

Chapter 9

1. Why is Mama frightened? (Mr. Wallace is making threats about people ruining his business.)

2. Was it okay for Cassie to do what she did to Lillian Jean?

3. Why did Stacey think what happened to Papa was his fault? (Because he was holding the horse's reins.)

adamant (203): unyielding

Chapter 10

1. Did Mr. Morrison put the Logan children in unfair danger when he moved Mr. Wallace's car?

2. Why did Cassie think T. J. was acting foolishly when he came to the revival? (Because of the way he was dressed and the way he acted.)

Chapter 11

1. What do you think the poem at the beginning of chapter 11 means? (Dissect the poem line by line, discussing the symbolism. For example, ask students to explain "The night whispered of distant thunder" (p. 185). Compare the poem, or part of the poem, to another resource, such as the books *Malcolm X, The People Could Fly, Hey Mom, Can I Ride My Bike Across America?* or the video *A Time for Justice.*

2. Do you think the fire will help to solve the problems between the African Americans and the whites? Why or why not?

3. How has Cassie's character changed over the course of the story? (Cassie is becoming more independent; she is learning when to fight against the racism that is so prevalent in her time.)

4. Why did Mildred Taylor decide to let Jeremy be the first one to feel the rain on the night of the fire? (He was innocent of the hatred held by other whites. People like Jeremy help to pave the road to change. It is hoped the fire will begin to build that road. To show Jeremy's relationship to change, he is the first to feel the rain.)

5. Discuss two events in *Roll of Thunder* that violate (go against) the "separate but equal" ruling from the 1896 case *Plessy* v. *Ferguson.* Use any events from the book. (The schoolhouse, the schoolbooks, the way the students get to school, where Big Ma had to park the wagon.)

6. How has racism affected Cassie and her family? (Profoundly—every aspect of their life.)

7. What examples of prejudice have you seen in your life?

8. Today, do poor and rich students receive equal education?

Reaching Out Through Reading Journal Reflections

Roll of Thunder, Hear My Cry

Chapter 1

1. In the first two chapters, what do you learn about Mississippi after the Civil War?
2. What is unusual about the land that Cassie lives on?
3. What is unusual about Jeremy?
4. Is Little Man giving himself "airs," as Miss Crocker claims on page 23?
5. Analyze the stamp found in Little Man's book on page 25. What would you have thought about or done if you were Little Man?
6. Was it right for Miss Crocker to switch Little Man and Cassie? What would you have done if you were Miss Crocker?
7. How did Cassie know her Mama understands about the books?

Chapters 2–3

1. Why is the book titled *Roll of Thunder, Hear My Cry*?
2. What do you think Mama meant when she told Mr. Morrison, "You're lucky no worse happened and we're glad to have you here . . . especially now"?
3. Using a dictionary to help you, define racism.
4. What are some examples of racism in this book?

Chapters 4–5

1. Stacey knew he could get into serious trouble if he fought with T. J., but he did it anyway. Was it worth it? Why?
2. What makes the land important to Big Ma?
3. What problems will the families face if they decide to shop in Vicksburg? List the problems discussed in chapter 4, and think about other problems they may face.
4. The Civil War has been over for some time. Why does Big Ma still have to park her wagon far away from the white parking areas?
5. Why do you think Cassie asked to be served after waiting so long?
6. Respond to the following quote from Mr. Barnett: " 'Get her out of here,' he said with hateful force, 'And make sure she don't come back till yo' mammy teach her what she is' " (p. 112).

7. Why did Big Ma make Cassie apologize to Lillian Jean? Why was it the right thing to do? Why was it the wrong thing to do?

Chapters 6–7

1. In your own words, explain what Mama told Cassie about why white people think they are better than African Americans. (Hint: Look on pages 126–130.)

2. What would you like to tell Cassie?

3. Why does Cassie believe Papa when he tells her they will never lose their land?

4. Why does Mr. Granger come to visit?

Chapters 8–9

1. Discuss two main reasons Mama was fired.

2. Respond to a passage of your choice from chapter 8.

3. Why is Mama frightened?

4. Was it okay for Cassie to do what she did to Lillian Jean?

5. Why did Stacey think what happened to Papa was his fault?

Chapters 10–11

1. Did Mr. Morrison put the Logan children in unfair danger when he moved Mr. Wallace's car?

2. Why did Cassie think T. J. was acting foolishly when he came to the revival?

3. What do you think the poem at the beginning of chapter 11 means?

4. Do you think the fire will help to solve the problems between the African Americans and the whites? Why or why not?

5. How has Cassie's character changed over the course of the story?

6. Why did Mildred Taylor decide to let Jeremy be the first one to feel the rain on the night of the fire?

7. Discuss two events in *Roll of Thunder* that violate (go against) the "separate but equal" ruling from the 1896 case *Plessy* v. *Ferguson*. Use any events from the book.

8. How has racism affected Cassie and her family?

9. What examples of prejudice have you seen in your life?

10. Today, do poor and rich students receive equal education?

From *Reaching Out Through Reading.* © 1998 Carrie Sorby Duits and Adelle K. Dorman. Teacher Ideas Press. (800) 237-6124.

Roll of Thunder, Hear My Cry
by Mildred D. Taylor

Name _____

Cut out the bus. On one side, write down some of the reasons that Mr. Granger might give for the discrimination that African Americans face in *Roll of Thunder, Hear My Cry*. On the other side of the bus, write down the reasons that Cassie would give for this discrimination.

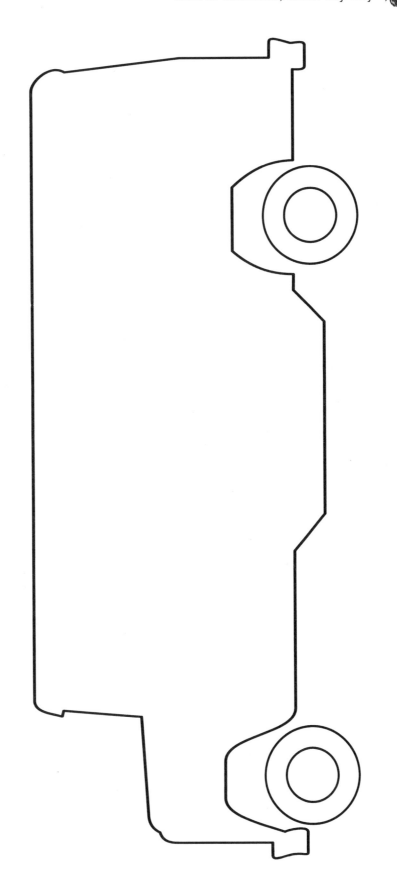

From *Reaching Out Through Reading*. © 1998 Carrie Sorby Duits and Adelle K. Dorman. Teacher Ideas Press. (800) 237-6124.

The Giver

Lois Lowry. New York: Bantam Doubleday Dell, 1993. 180 pages.
Intermediate grade levels.

At the beginning of *The Giver*, the reader is introduced to Jonas, an 11-year-old boy living in an extremely unusual community. Jonas waits anxiously for the Ceremony of Twelve, in which he will be given the Assignment that will dictate his life's work. When the time finally comes, Jonas is given the most honored Assignment in the community, Receiver of Memory. During his training, Jonas and his trainer, the Giver, come to regard the community and its secrets with contempt and pity. Jonas escapes, and the result is freeing of memory from the past. Jonas's flight from the community is long and difficult, but in the end he finds peace.

Some important messages to gain from this book are:

❖ The importance of individuality.

❖ The importance of community as a support system.

❖ The importance of the roles of people in their government.

❖ Being allowed to make mistakes helps people grow.

ACTIVITY BRIDGE TO SERVICE LEARNING

Give students a copy of *The Giver* worksheet (page 178) after they read chapter 6. On the right side of the worksheet have them describe Jonas's community at this point in the book. On the left side of the worksheet, have them describe what Jonas believes is an ideal community at this point in the book. Have students repeat the exercise, using the same worksheet, after they read chapters 17 and 21.

After finishing the book, have students gather as a class (with their completed worksheets). Using butcher paper to record student responses, ask students to describe what they think their community should be like. After students have had an opportunity to share their thoughts, draw a line on the paper. Then, ask students to describe what their community is like. Record their answers below the line. Look for discrepancies between what students would like their community to be and what it is. Use these discrepancies to open student discussion of opportunities for service learning within their community. Allow students to choose an area of service they would like to pursue.

Suggested service learning projects

Develop a list of questions the class could ask elderly people to learn more about the past. Visit a nursing home and ask patients to tell stories and answer questions. Write their stories and make a history book for the school library.

Write to your state representatives to voice concern about an issue in your community.

Visit your state congress. Share what you learn with younger students.

Make a living journal to trade with another class in a different part of the country. Try to represent your class and your community through video, pictures, writing, and artifacts.

As a class or in small groups, brainstorm things students would like to change in their community. Select one idea and pursue a way to make the change happen.

Related literature

Andersen, Hans Christian. *The Nightingale.* New York: Crown, 1985.

Blumberg, Rhoda. *Bloomers!* New York: Bradbury Press, 1993.

Bunting, Eve. *How Many Days to America?* New York: Clarion Books, 1988.

Carrick, Donald. *Herald and the Great Stag.* New York: Clarion Books, 1988.

Fleishman, Paul. *Bull Run.* New York: Harper Trophy, 1993.

Fleishman, Sid. *The Whipping Boy.* New York: Greenwillow Books, 1986.

Johnston, Tony. *The Wagon.* New York: Tambourine Books, 1996.

Kennedy, John. *Profiles in Courage.* New York: Harper & Row, 1956.

Lomask, Milton. *The Spirit of 1787: The Making of Our Constitution.* New York: Fawcett Juniper, 1980.

Lukes, Bonnie. *The American Revolution.* San Diego: Lucent Books, 1996.

McCully, Emily. *Staring Mirette and Bellini.* New York: G. P. Putnam's Sons, 1997.

Small, David. *Ruby Mae Has Something to Say.* New York: Crown, 1992.

Discussion questions and vocabulary

Chapter 1

1. Why do you think Jonas was feeling apprehensive about the Ceremony of Twelve? (It would determine his occupation.)

2. When have you felt apprehensive about something?

3. Why did Lily think the other group of Sevens acted like animals? (Because they acted differently.)

4. What do you think it means to be released from the community?

dwelling (2): a place where one lives

distraught (4): upset

recollection (4): a memory

apprehensive (4): worried and hesitant

defiant (5): rebellious

disposition (7): attitude

transgression (9): breaking a rule or taboo

Chapter 2

1. Should Father have broken the rule to learn Gabriel's name?

2. How did Father and Mother try to reassure Jonas? (They told him about their own experiences.)

3. Why were the elephant and bear comfort objects referred to as imaginary? (They do not exist in the community's memory.)

adherence (12): closely following instructions

assembled (13): gathered together

impatient (13): restlessly eager

aptitude (15): potential ability

affectionately (19): with care and tenderness

Chapter 3

1. What does Jonas have in common with the newchild? Why do you think this is rare in the community? (Jonas and the newchild both have light-colored eyes. This is rare because having light eyes is a recessive trait.)

2. Why does the assignment of Birthmother hold little honor? (Females are Birthmothers for only a short time, and then they become laborers.)

3. Describe Jonas's experience with the apple. Make a guess about what happened. (It changed.)

chastise (20): verbally punish

petulantly (22): irritably

acknowledged (22): admitted

reluctantly (22): with reservation, halfheartedly

humiliation (23): embarrassment or shame

hoarded (23): stored away greedily

remorse (23): sadness and regret

reflective (25): thoughtful

solemn (25): serious

Chapter 4

1. Why doesn't Jonas have any idea what his Assignment will be? (Because he worked his volunteer hours in a variety of places.)

2. What is the release of the Old like? (The elderly are honored in a ceremony.)

confided (31): told privately, usually a secret

Chapter 5

1. Why did Jonas feel proud when he started taking the pills? (Taking the pills meant he had become an adult.)

ritual (34): ceremony

disquieting (34): unsettling

reassuring (38): comforting

Chapter 6

1. Why was Caleb's naming special? (He was replacing another boy named Caleb who died.)
2. How do you feel about people in the community being assigned spouses and newchildren?

irritably (40): crankily, easily upset

interdependence (40): need for each other

emblem (41): symbol

throng (41): huge crowd

cringed (45): cowered, flinched with fear

summoned (45): called up

violation (46): crime, invasion, breaking rules

merriment (47): celebration

scrupulously (49): ethically

Chapter 7

1. Name five things Jonas must have been feeling when he was skipped at the Ceremony of Twelve. (Anxiety, failure, surprise, fear, worry, dismay, etc.)
2. Why do you think Jonas was skipped?

irritation (50): annoyance

profound (51): important

standardize (51): to make the same

prestige (53): public importance

self-consciously (53): shyly

acquisition (54): gain

Chapter 8

1. What is the difference between being assigned and being selected? (Being selected happens rarely and only for honored positions.)
2. Why did the community chant Jonas's name? (It was acknowledging his selection.)

crescendo (59): peak

kinship (59): close friendship

humiliation (59): embarrassment

vibrant (59): energetic or colorful

gracious (59): thankful, kind, and courteous

anguish (50): pain

intently (61): with concentration

unanimous (62): all in agreement

integrity (62): going along with a code of values

gratitude (64): a feeling of thankfulness

Chapter 9

1. Why is Asher acting differently toward Jonas? (Jonas has been selected to perform a very special job.)

2. Which rules of Jonas's assignment startle you the most? Why?

hesitation (65): a brief delay

relish (68): enjoy greatly

dismayed (69): upset or worried

excruciating (70): very intense (usually to describe pain)

empowered (71): given an ability

Chapter 10

1. What do you think about one person being responsible for holding the memories of the whole world?

2. How would you feel if you were Jonas?

3. What question would you want to ask the Giver?

4. Why must the Giver lose memories when he gives them to Jonas? (Otherwise, two people would have the same memory, which is not what the community wants.)

tentatively (77): possibly, but not surely

astonishing (79): amazing

betray (79): be unfaithful to

Chapter 11

consciousness (86): mental awareness

Chapter 12

1. Why wouldn't Jonas be able to describe his new job, even if he was allowed to talk about it? (His job involves things that no one else in the community would understand.)

2. What is your opinion about the discipline wand?

3. Do you think the community made the right decision when it went to Sameness?

4. What has the community gained by going to Sameness? What has it lost? (Gains: Freedom from discrimination, hunger, war, and poverty. Losses: Individuality, free choice, feelings.)

fretful (88): worried

significant (88): important

admonition (89): scolding

indescribable (90): impossible to put into words

phenomenon (91): occurrence

dumbfounded (93): mentally stunned

Chapter 13

1. Respond to the following quote from the book:

   "We really have to protect people from wrong choices."
   "It's safer."
   "Yes," Jonas agreed. "Much safer."

   What do you think?

2. Jonas is angry because his groupmates are happy. Why? (Because they can't truly feel.)

3. Why could it be dangerous for Jonas to try to give Asher an understanding of color and Lily an understanding of elephants? (They wouldn't know how to handle the new information and the feelings they engendered.)

4. Why doesn't the community want change? (Change would bring pain and sorrow as well as good things.)

hueless (97): colorless, not well defined

anguished (100): extremely pained

indifferently (101): without care

Chapter 14

1. Why can't Jonas have relief-of-pain? (He must experience pain to receive the memories.)

2. Why does it make Jonas feel lonely to know that his family has never experienced pain? (They cannot empathize with his feelings.)

3. How is Jonas serving his community? (By holding the memories of the past, he allows the community to be unburdened.)

4. Why doesn't the community share memories, instead of having one Receiver? (The community doesn't want to be burdened with the memories; the community values sameness.)

5. Why do you think that no twins are allowed in the community when the community works so hard at sameness?

6. Do you think Jonas made the right decision to *not* tell the Giver about giving the memory to Gabriel?

ominous (113): threatening

placidly (114): calmly

Chapter 15

1. Why did the Giver say "forgive me" at the end of the chapter? (Because a memory he gave Jonas caused Jonas pain.)

carnage (119): large-scale killing

grotesquely (119): horribly

crimson (119): blood-red

imploring (119): begging

Chapter 16

1. Why did Mother and Father think it was funny when Jonas asked them if they loved him? (They didn't feel that the term *love* held meaning.)
2. Why did Jonas throw his pill away? (Because he wanted to feel.)

unique (121): one of a kind

ecstatic (122): extremely happy

perceive (123): understand

optimistic (128): positive outlook

Chapter 17

1. Comment about the following quote:
   "Jonas knew with certainty that he could change nothing" (p. 135).

analyzed (131): carefully thought over

exasperation (132): frustration

suppressing (133): keeping down

Chapter 18

1. Describe Rosemary. (She is brave, female, Giver loved her, she applied for release.)
2. Did Rosemary fail in her training?
3. How would you end the story?

dejected (139): low spirited

self-possessed (140): self-confident

successor (143): next to take a position

devastated (144): destroyed

Chapter 19

1. Why do you think the Giver talked Jonas into viewing the release of the twin? (The Giver wants Jonas to understand what really happens in the community.)
2. Was Rosemary brave to ask for release?
3. How does Jonas feel now that he knows what his father does during a release? (He feels betrayed and anguished.)

wretched (151): very distressed

Chapter 20

1. Why does Jonas suggest that he and the Giver don't need to care about the others? Why does he change his mind?

2. Do you think the plan will work?

3. What does the Giver mean when he says that after his work is done, he wants to be with his daughter? (He wants to be released.)

mimicked (152): imitated

sarcastic (152): said in a cruel, mocking way

emphatically (157): with stress

inconsiderate (158): thoughtless

solace (161): relief

Chapter 21

1. Why did the plan change? (Gabriel was going to be released the next morning.)

2. Was Jonas right to take Gabe?

3. What will happen to Jonas if he is caught? (He will be killed.)

4. Why did Jonas make himself and Gabe cold? (So the planes' heat-seeking devices could not detect them.)

5. How did Jonas serve his community by leaving? (His leaving forced the community to accept its memories.)

Chapter 22

1. What sort of new things did Jonas encounter on his journey? (Animals, hills, changes in weather.)

2. What has become Jonas's biggest fear? (Starvation.)

3. How would Jonas have starved if he had remained in the community? (He would have starved for love, feelings, and variety or differences.)

4. Why did Jonas cry? (He didn't think he could save Gabriel.)

tentatively (171): cautiously

diminished (171): made smaller or fewer

awed (172): amazed and impressed

exquisite (172): wonderful

cultivated (172): grew or tended to, developed

yearned (174): longed for

Chapter 23

1. What is keeping Jonas alive? (Hope and scraps of memories.)
2. Does Jonas actually hear music, or is it only an echo?
3. Do you think Jonas survived the journey? Explain your answer.

imperceptibly (176): subtly, without notice   **resignation** (177): giving up
lethargy (177): tiredness

Reaching Out Through Reading Journal Reflections

The Giver

Chapters 1–2

1. Why do you think Jonas was feeling apprehensive about the Ceremony of Twelve?
2. When have you felt apprehensive about something?
3. Why did Lily think the other group of Sevens acted like animals?
4. What do you think it means to be released from the community?
5. Should Father have broken the rule to learn Gabriel's name?
6. How did Father and Mother try to reassure Jonas?
7. Why were the elephant and bear comfort objects referred to as imaginary?

Chapters 3–5

1. What does Jonas have in common with the newchild? Why do you think this is rare in the community?
2. Why does the assignment of Birthmother hold little honor?
3. Describe Jonas's experience with the apple. Make a guess about what happened.
4. Why doesn't Jonas have any idea what his Assignment will be?
5. What is the release of the Old like?
6. Why did Jonas feel proud when he started taking the pills?

Chapters 6–8

1. Why was Caleb's naming special?
2. How do you feel about people in the community being assigned spouses and new children?
3. Name five things Jonas must have been feeling when he was skipped at the Ceremony of Twelve.
4. Why do you think Jonas was skipped?
5. What is the difference between being assigned and being selected?
6. Why did the community chant Jonas's name?

From *Reaching Out Through Reading*. © 1998 Carrie Sorby Duits and Adelle K. Dorman. Teacher Ideas Press. (800) 237-6124.

Chapters 9–12

1. Why is Asher acting differently toward Jonas?
2. Which rules of Jonas's assignment startle you the most? Why?
3. What do you think about one person being responsible for holding the memories of the whole world?
4. How would you feel if you were Jonas?
5. What question would you want to ask the Giver?
6. Why must the Giver lose memories when he gives them to Jonas?
7. Why wouldn't Jonas be able to describe his new job, even if he was allowed to talk about it?
8. What is your opinion about the discipline wand?
9. Do you think the community made the right decision when it went to Sameness?
10. What has the community gained by going to Sameness? What has it lost?

Chapters 13–14

1. Respond to the following quote:

   "We really have to protect people from wrong choices."
   "It's safer."
   "Yes," Jonas agreed. "Much safer."

   What do you think?
2. Jonas is angry because his groupmates are happy. Why?
3. Why could it be dangerous for Jonas to try to give Asher an understanding of color and Lily an understanding of elephants?
4. Why doesn't the community want change?
5. Why can't Jonas have relief-of-pain?
6. Why does it make Jonas feel lonely to know that his family has never experienced pain?
7. How is Jonas serving his community?
8. Why doesn't the community share memories, instead of having one Receiver?
9. Why do you think that no twins are allowed in the community when the community works so hard at sameness?
10. Do you think Jonas made the right decision to *not* tell the Giver about giving the memory to Gabriel?

Chapters 15–17

1. Why did the Giver say "forgive me" at the end of the chapter?
2. Why did Mother and Father think it was funny when Jonas asked if they loved him?

From *Reaching Out Through Reading*. © 1998 Carrie Sorby Duits and Adelle K. Dorman. Teacher Ideas Press. (800) 237-6124.

3. Why did Jonas throw his pill away?
4. Comment about the following quote:
   "Jonas knew with certainty that he could change nothing" (p. 135).

Chapters 18–19

1. Describe Rosemary.
2. Did Rosemary fail in her training?
3. How would you end the story?
4. Why do you think the Giver talked Jonas into viewing the release of the twin?
5. Was Rosemary brave to ask for release?
6. How does Jonas feel now that he knows what his father does during a release?

Chapters 20–21

1. Why does Jonas suggest that he and the Giver don't need to care about the others? Why does he change his mind?
2. Do you think the plan will work?
3. What does the Giver mean when he says that after his work is done, he wants to be with his daughter?
4. Why did the plan change?
5. Was Jonas right to take Gabe?
6. What will happen to Jonas if he is caught?
7. Why did Jonas make himself and Gabe cold?
8. How did Jonas serve his community by leaving?

Chapters 22–23

1. What sort of new things did Jonas encounter on his journey?
2. What has become Jonas's biggest fear?
3. How would Jonas have starved if he had remained in the community?
4. Why did Jonas cry?
5. What is keeping Jonas alive?
6. Does Jonas actually hear music, or is it only an echo?
7. Do you think Jonas survived the journey? Explain your answer.

From *Reaching Out Through Reading*. © 1998 Carrie Sorby Duits and Adelle K. Dorman. Teacher Ideas Press. (800) 237-6124.

The Giver
by Lois Lowry

Name _____

Describe Jonas's community.

Chapter 6: _____

Chapter 6: _____

Chapter 17: _____

Chapter 21: _____

Chapter 17: _____

Chapter 21: _____

Describe what Jonas thinks a community should be.

From *Reaching Out Through Reading.* © 1998 Carrie Sorby Duits and Adelle K. Dorman. Teacher Ideas Press. (800) 237-6124.

Part 3

Service Learning Toolkit

Resources for Service Learning

Reproducibles for Service Learning

RESOURCES FOR SERVICE LEARNING

When designing a service learning project, think globally and act locally. Exploring local possibilities for service allows students to become involved in their own community. The government listings and the business listings in the local telephone directory are valuable first resources for developing service learning projects.

The resources here will help you develop service learning projects related to the books highlighted in part 2. Organizations, clearinghouses, and resource books are listed in this chapter. It should be noted that the books listed in this chapter are volunteer resource books; they do not make the academic connection required in true service learning projects.

LOCAL CONTACTS FOR SERVICE LEARNING PROJECTS

Use a local directory to find telephone numbers and addresses for:

Animal shelters
Community centers
Day care centers
Fire departments
Food banks
Homeless shelters
Hospitals
Human services departments
Meals on Wheels
Museums

Nursing homes
Parks and recreation departments
Preschools
Rehabilitation centers
Safe houses
Schools and educational programs
Senior citizen centers
Voter registration organizations
Zoos

National Service Organizations

Contact the volunteer coordinator to ask about resources or ways your class can provide a service for these organizations.

Animals

Literature Connections: *The Lorax; Sarah, Plain and Tall; Stone Fox; The Trumpet of the Swan; Smoky Night; Knots on a Counting Rope.*

American Humane Association
P.O. Box 1266
Denver, CO 80201
1-303-792-9900
The American Humane Association is an animal rights organization. Its work includes educational programs about animal safety and animal care.

Delta Society
321 Burnett Ave. S., Third Floor
Renton, WA 98055-2569
1-206-226-7357
The Delta Society promotes human health and therapy through interactions with animals and nature.

National Audubon Society
Christmas Bird Count
950 Third Ave.
New York, NY 10022
1-212-832-3200
The National Audubon Society is a conservation association concerned with the environment and wildlife.

Pacific Whale Foundation
101 N. Kihei Rd., Suite 21
Kihei, Maui, HI 96753-8833
1-800-WHALE-11
The Pacific Whale Foundation promotes education on the ocean and marine life.

People for the Ethical Treatment of Animals
P.O. Box 42516
Washington, DC 20015-0516
1-301-770-7382
People for the Ethical Treatment of Animals works to defend the rights of animals.

The Arts

Literature Connections: *From the Mixed-Up Files of Mrs. Basil E. Frankweiler; The Patchwork Quilt; The Switching Well.*

ABC Quilts
P.O. Box 107
Weatherford, OK 73096
1-405-772-2229
ABC Quilts collects and distributes handmade quilts for AIDS babies.

American Association of Museum Volunteers
1225 I St., NW, Suite 200
Washington, DC 20005
1-202-289-1818
The American Association of Museum Volunteers has a clearinghouse that can provide information about volunteering in museums.

The NAMES Project AIDS Memorial Quilt
2362 Market St.
San Francisco, CA 94114
1-914-863-5511
The NAMES Project AIDS Memorial Quilt is a symbol remembering those who have died of AIDS. Volunteers can make a panel for the Quilt, display the Quilt, or hold a quilting bee for the Quilt.

National Assembly of Local Arts Agencies
927 15th St., NW, 12th Floor
Washington, DC 20005
1-202-371-2830
The National Assembly of Local Arts Agencies
provides funding and help for local art agencies.

At-Risk Youth

Literature Connections: *Roll of Thunder, Hear
My Cry; Dragonwings; We Are All in the
Dumps with Jack and Guy.*

Magic Me
808 N. Charles St.
Baltimore, MD 21201
1-301-837-0900
Magic Me matches volunteer students with
at-risk children.

Disabilities

Literature Connections: *Now One Foot, Now the
Other; The Switching Well; Knots on a Counting
Rope; The Trumpet of the Swan; Dragonwings.*

Arthritis Foundation
P.O. Box 19000
Atlanta, GA 30326
1-800-283-7800
The Arthritis Foundation provides resource
centers for people with arthritis. They also
use volunteers for educational programs,
recreation projects, and fund-raising.

March of Dimes Birth Defects Foundation
1275 Mamaroneck Ave.
White Plains, NY 10605
1-914-428-7100
The March of Dimes Birth Defects Foundation promotes research, education, and community services to improve the health of
babies and to prevent birth defects.

National Society to Prevent Blindness
500 E. Remington Rd.
Schaumburg, IL 60173
1-708-843-2020
The National Society to Prevent Blindness
provides blindness-prevention programs.

*Promote Real Independence for the
      Disabled and Elderly*
1159 Poquonnock Rd.
Groton, CT 06340
1-203-447-7433
Promote Real Independence for the Disabled and Elderly sponsors educational programs and home services for the disabled.

Disaster Services

Literature Connections: *Dragonwings; Roll of
Thunder, Hear My Cry; Smoky Night.*

American Red Cross Disaster Services
17th and D Streets, NW
Washington, DC 20006
1-202-737-8300
The American Red Cross helps disaster victims and provides emergency services.

AmeriCares Foundation
161 Cherry St.
New Canaan, CT 06840
1-203-966-5195
The AmeriCares Foundation provides relief
for medical and nutritional emergencies
around the world.

The United Way of America
701 N. Fairfax St.
Alexandria, VA 22314
1-703-836-7100
The main focus of The United Way of America is to support critical local issues and
services in order to build stronger, healthier
communities.

Education

Literature Connections: *Sarah, Plain and Tall; Roll of Thunder, Hear My Cry; The Hundred Penny Box; From the Mixed-Up Files of Mrs. Basil E. Frankweiler; The Hundred Dresses; Smoky Night.*

American Association of University Women
1111 16th St., NW
Washington, DC 20036
1-202-785-7700
The American Association of University Women promotes the fair treatment and education of women and girls.

Reading Is Fundamental
Smithsonian Institution
600 Maryland Ave., NW, Suite 500
Washington, DC 20560
1-202-287-3220
Reading Is Fundamental encourages young people to read by allowing them to select and keep a book of their own.

The Elderly

Literature Connections: *Now One Foot, Now the Other; The Patchwork Quilt; Stone Fox; The Hundred Penny Box; Knots on a Counting Rope.*

FOSTER GRANDPARENT PROGRAM
ACTION
1100 Vermont Ave., NW
Washington, DC 20525
1-202-606-4855
The Foster Grandparent Program matches elderly volunteers with special-needs children.

National Council of Senior Citizens
925 15th St., NW
Washington, DC 20005
1-202-347-8800
The National Council of Senior Citizens supports the elderly by addressing issues they face.

The Environment

Literature Connections: *The Lorax; The Giving Tree; Stone Fox; Sarah, Plain and Tall.*

American Forestry Association
P.O. Box 2000
Washington, DC 20013
1-202-667-3300
The American Forestry Association is involved with environmental conservation.

American Free Tree Program
P.O. Box 9079
Canton, OH 44711
1-216-456-TREE
The American Free Tree Program distributes free trees for projects across the United States.

Earth First!
P.O. Box 5176
Missoula, MT 59806
Earth First! is an organization whose main goal is to preserve wilderness areas.

National Arbor Day Foundation
100 Arbor Ave.
Nebraska City, NE 68410
1-402-474-5655
The National Arbor Day Foundation provides Arbor Day information and free trees for planting.

Rainforest Action Network
450 Broadway, Suite 700
San Francisco, CA 94111
1-415-398-4404
The Rainforest Action Network is committed to saving tropical rainforests.

Sierra Club
730 Polk St.
San Francisco, CA 94109
1-415-923-5630
The Sierra Club sponsors wilderness projects.

Student Conservation Association
National Office
P.O. Box 550
Charlestown, NH 03603
1-603-832-4301
The Student Conservation Association helps to maintain national parks.

TreePeople
12601 Mulholland Dr.
Beverly Hills, CA 90210
1-818-753-4600
TreePeople encourages environmental awareness through tree planting.

U.S. Department of Agriculture, Forest Service
Human Resource Programs
12th St. and Independence Ave., SW
P.O. Box 96090
Washington, DC 20090-6090
1-703-235-8855
The U.S. Department of Agriculture maintains national forests.

U.S. Department of the Interior
National Park Service Volunteers in Parks
1849 C St., NW
Washington, DC 20240
1-202-208-3100
The U.S. Department of the Interior matches volunteers with national park services.

Human Rights/Peace Efforts

Literature Connections: *Dragonwings; The Giver; Roll of Thunder, Hear My Cry.*

Amnesty International USA
National Office
322 8th Ave.
New York, NY 10001
1-212-807-8400
The goal of Amnesty International USA is to release people who have been imprisoned because of their beliefs, color, gender, religion, or ethnicity.

Children as the Peacemakers
999 Green St.
San Francisco, CA 94133
1-415-775-2323
Children as the Peacemakers allows students to play an active part in peace efforts through cultural exchange and communication with world leaders.

Illness or Death

Literature Connections: *The Velveteen Rabbit; Now One Foot, Now the Other; Taste of Blackberries; Sadako and the Thousand Paper Cranes; Stone Fox; Roll of Thunder, Hear My Cry; The Patchwork Quilt.*

American Cancer Society
1599 Clifton Rd., NE
Atlanta, GA 30329
1-800-227-2345
The American Cancer Society has service programs for cancer patients and their families and educational programs for the detection and prevention of cancer.

American Heart Association
7272 Greenville Ave.
Dallas, TX 75231-4596
1-800-242-8721
One goal of the American Heart Association is to present educational programs that teach students about the heart.

International Child Health Foundation
American City Bldg.
P.O. Box 1205
Columbia, MD 21044
1-301-596-4514
The International Child Health Foundation emphasizes better health care for children by preventing and treating diseases.

Mail for Tots
P.O. Box 8699
Boston, MA 02114
1-617-242-3538

Mail for Tots asks volunteers to send friendly letters to seriously ill children.

Make-a-Wish Foundation of America
National Office
2600 N. Central Ave., Suite 936
Phoenix, AZ 85004
1-800-722-WISH
The Make-a-Wish Foundation grants wishes to seriously ill children.

Ronald McDonald House
500 N. Michigan Ave., Suite 200
Chicago, IL 60611
1-313-836-7104
The Ronald McDonald House supports families of seriously ill children by providing a place for them to stay when their children need treatment far away from home.

Immigrants

Literature Connections: *Dragonwings; The Hundred Dresses.*

American Council for Nationalities Service
National Headquarters
95 Madison Ave.
New York, NY 10016
1-212-532-5858
The American Council for Nationalities Service helps immigrants settle in their new communities.

Refugee Voices
3041 4th St., NE
Washington, DC 20017-1102
1-202-832-0020
Refugee Voices sponsors radio shows for refugees. You can obtain information about local agencies that help refugees through this organization.

U.S. Department of Justice
Immigration and Naturalization Service
Examinations Operations Facilitation
  Program
425 I St., NW
Washington, DC 20536
1-202-633-4123
The U.S. Department of Justice helps people who have moved to the United States and are having problems resettling.

Minorities

Literature Connections: *Roll of Thunder, Hear My Cry; Dragonwings; Knots on a Counting Rope; The Switching Well; The Hundred Dresses; Stone Fox; The Patchwork Quilt; Smoky Night.*

American Indian Heritage Foundation
6051 Arlington Blvd.
Falls Church, VA 22044
1-202-INDIANS
The American Indian Heritage Foundation provides social and economic relief and development for Native Americans.

National Council of La Raza
810 1st St., NE, Suite 300
Washington, DC 20003-4205
1-202-289-1380
The National Council of La Raza strengthens the Latino community through education.

National Council of Negro Women, Inc.
1211 Connecticut Ave., NW, Suite 702
Washington, DC 20036
1-202-659-2372
The National Council of Negro Women, Inc., provides services for African American women in need.

Substance Abuse

Literature Connections: *Dragonwings; The Switching Well; We Are All in the Dumps with Jack and Guy; The Giver.*

Mothers Against Drunk Driving
511 E. Carpenter Freeway, Suite 700
Irving, TX 75062-8187
1-800-GET-MADD
MADD encourages community participation to eliminate drunk driving.

Partnership for a Drug-Free America
666 Third Ave.
New York, NY 10017
1-212-922-1560
The Partnership for a Drug-Free America works for community education to prevent substance abuse.

Support Services

Literature Connections: *It Takes a Village; We Are All in the Dumps with Jack and Guy; The Hundred Dresses; Stone Fox; Smoky Night; The Giving Tree; The Switching Well; Roll of Thunder, Hear My Cry; Dragonwings.*

Conflict Resolution Center International, Inc.
7101 Hamilton Ave.
Pittsburgh, PA 15208-1828
1-415-371-9884
Conflict Resolution Center International, Inc., helps to resolve conflicts and disputes by providing a resource center and clearinghouse.

For the Love of Children
1711 14th St., NW
Washington, DC 20009
1-202-462-8686
For the Love of Children addresses child welfare issues.

Habitat for Humanity International, Inc.
Habitat and Church Streets
Americus, GA 31709-3498
1-912-924-6935
Habitat for Humanity International, Inc., builds houses for low-income families.

U.S. National Committee for World Food Day
1001 22nd St., NW
Washington, DC 20437
1-202-653-2404
The U.S. National Committee for World Food Day can provide information and materials for sponsoring a World Food Day.

USA Harvest
P.O. Box 1628
Louisville, KY 40201-1628
1-800-872-4366
USA Harvest feeds the hungry by collecting surplus food and distributing it among non-profit agencies.

Veterans

Literature Connections: *Sadako and the Thousand Paper Cranes.*

American Legion
National Headquarters
P.O. Box 1055
700 N. Pennsylvania St.
Indianapolis, IN 46206
1-317-635-8411
The American Legion supports education and community activities.

Disabled American Veterans
807 Main Ave., SW
Washington, DC 20024
1-202-554-3501
The Disabled American Veterans sponsors employment, emergency disaster relief, and scholarships for children of disabled veterans.

Volunteer Clearinghouses

ACCESS: Networking in the Public Interest
50 Beacon St.
Boston, MA 02108
1-617-720-5627

ACTION
Office of Public Affairs
1100 Vermont Ave., NW
Washington, DC 20525
1-202-606-5108

American Association of Retired Persons
601 E St., NW
Washington, DC 20049
1-202-434-2277

National Hospice Organization
1901 N. Moore St., Suite 901
Arlington, VA 22209
1-703-243-5900

Volunteer Resource Books

Angus, Susan, ed. *Invest Yourself.* New York: The Commission on Voluntary Service and Action, 1991.

Carroll, Andrew, and Christopher Miller. *Volunteer USA!* New York: Fawcett Columbine, 1991.

Driver, David E. *The Good Heart Book: A Guide to Volunteering.* Chicago: The Noble Press, 1989.

Knipe, Judy. *Stand Up and Be Counted: The Volunteer Resource Book.* New York: Simon & Schuster, 1992.

Terry, Max, ed. *Volunteer! The Comprehensive Guide to Voluntary Service in the U.S. and Abroad.* New York: Council on International Educational Exchange and Council of Religious Volunteer Agencies, 1992.

Woodworth, David. *The International Directory of Volunteer Work.* Oxford, England: Vacation Work, 1993.

REPRODUCIBLES FOR SERVICE LEARNING

The reproducible tools in this chapter facilitate the development of the service learning project. They include graphic organizers for brainstorming; communication aids, such as form letters and a telephone script; and project evaluations.

Three-Column Brainstorming

Your Interests	Important Messages from the Book	Service Possibilities

The Web to Service

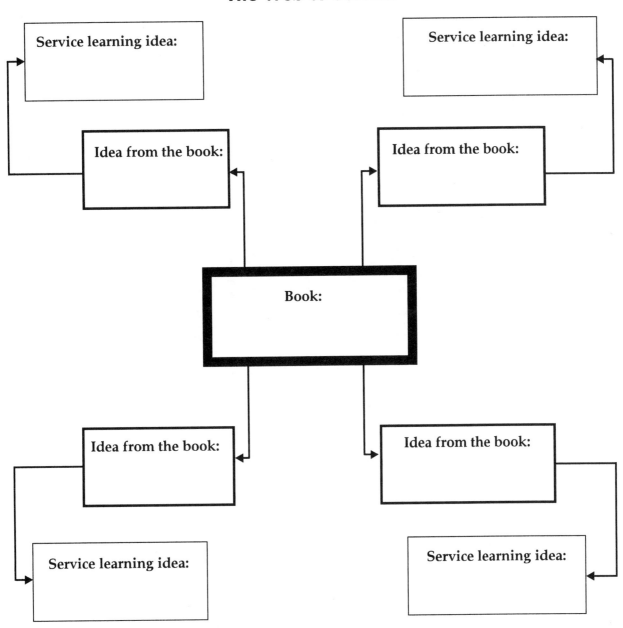

Three-Way Journal Response

Issue or Quote from the Book	Community Issue or Response to Quote	Possible Service Learning Project

Reflective Windows

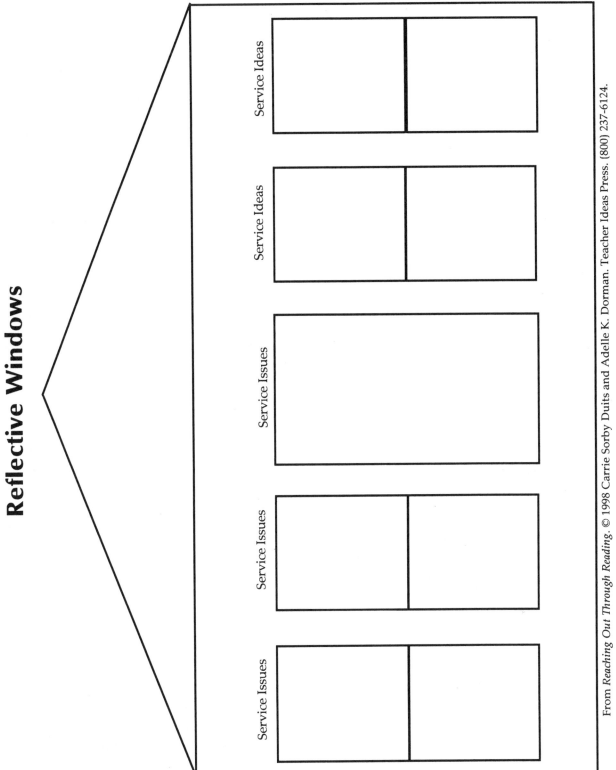

Service Ideas

Service Ideas

Service Issues

Service Issues

Service Issues

From *Reaching Out Through Reading*. © 1998 Carrie Sorby Duits and Adelle K. Dorman. Teacher Ideas Press. (800) 237-6124.

Project Discussion Frame

What is the name of the project?				
How would we carry out the project?				
Do we have all of the resources needed to do the project?				
When would the project take place?				
What would we learn from doing the project?				

From *Reaching Out Through Reading*. © 1998 Carrie Sorby Duits and Adelle K. Dorman. Teacher Ideas Press. (800) 237-6124.

From Character Needs to Community Needs

Book Title:

Characters in the book:

What problems do the characters face?

If I were a character in the book, what could I do to help?

Who do I know in my community that needs help? What could the class do to help?

Project Planner

Service Learning Project Title:

What will we do?
Whom will we be serving?

What will we need in order to do the project?

How will we get permission to do the project?
❖ Principal Support Letter
❖
❖

What will we learn by doing the project?

Project Details

What are the steps we need to take in order to do this project?	Who will be responsible for the steps of the project?	By when will each step need to be accomplished?

Project Time Line

Write the target dates in the top row of the time line. Decide who will be responsible for the various steps of the project. Write their names in the left column. In the body of the chart, identify the steps of the service learning project in the correct space according to who will be responsible for the step and when. Note: You may need more than one time line to schedule all the steps in your project. Complete this time line in pencil. It will probably change as the project develops!

Student Names	Date	Date	Date	Date	Date

Letter to Ask for Information (Template)

Your Name
Name of Your School
Street Address
City, State Zip Code
Date

The Name of the Person Receiving This Letter
Job Title
Company Name
Street Address
City, State Zip Code

The Name of the Person Receiving This Letter:

In the opening paragraph, state who you are and what you are doing.

In the body of the letter, explain what information you need and what you will do with the information. Be specific.

In the closing paragraph, explain the importance of your request. Also, thank the person you are addressing for his or her time and consideration.

Sincerely,

Your Name
Your Grade in School

Letter to Ask for Information (Sample)

Sally Swan
Service Learning Elementary School
1234 Caring Way
Denver, CO 80000
Oct. 11, 1997

Sam Beaver
Zookeeper
All City Zoo
1234 Koho Ave.
Denver, CO 80000

Dear Mr. Beaver:

I am a fifth-grade student at Service Learning Elementary School. My classmates and I have been reading *The Trumpet of the Swan* by E. B. White. We are very interested in sponsoring a bird in your zoo or endangered birds in the wild.

Please send us any information that you have about endangered birds. We will be using the information to design our service learning project.

If you have any other ideas about how we can help save endangered birds, we would appreciate hearing them. We know that birds are an important part of the ecosystem and we want to do what we can to save birds. Thank you for your time and help.

Sincerely,

Sally Swan

Thank-You Letter

Date

Dear _____ ,

In the opening paragraph, thank the person for their help. Be specific.

In the body of the letter, tell about the project and how it was improved by the help you received from this person.

In the closing paragraph, restate your appreciation.

Sincerely,

Your Name
Your Grade in School
The Name of Your School

From *Reaching Out Through Reading*. © 1998 Carrie Sorby Duits and Adelle K. Dorman. Teacher Ideas Press. (800) 237-6124.

Letter Asking for the Principal's Support

Dear Mr./Ms. (Principal's name) _____ ,

(Teacher's name) _____ 's class is considering doing a service learning project focusing on _____. For this project, we will be serving the community by doing _____. We hope to learn about _____. This project will take about (hours, days, weeks, months) _____. Please let our class know if you have any questions or concerns about this project.

Thank you,

Your Name(s)

Your Grade

Phone Script

To the person who answers the phone say:

Hello. My name is _____

from _____ School. May I please speak

with _____ (contact's name) or your volunteer coordinator?

Be prepared for the following responses:
If the response is:
She/He is not here right now.
You say:

May I leave a message? I'm calling to get information about volunteering. My phone number

is _____ (school phone number) and my teacher's name

is _____ .

or
If the response is:
May I ask why you are calling?
You say:

I'm calling to get information about volunteering for your organization.

When you are connected to your contact or the volunteer coordinator, say:

Hello. My name is _____ from

_____ School. I am calling because . . . (State

the purpose of your call. Example: My class is designing a project to help the elderly.)

If the response is:
What is your question? or How can I help you? or What do you need?
You say: [Here you will need to be prepared to ask for what you would like to know, for example, "Are there any ways students can help or volunteer for your organization?" or "How would we get started? Can you send us additional information?"]

Notes: Be sure to write important information during the phone call. Ask your contact to repeat information or to wait while you jot your notes. They will be happy to help you get it right!

Thank you for your help. I will share this call with my class and teacher. Goodbye.

The name of the person to whom you spoke: _____

Date of call: _____

Reflection Summary

What did we do?

What was my part in the project?

What did I learn?

How was the project important to me?

How was the project important to others?

On the back of this piece of paper, draw a special memory of the service learning project.

Reflective Evaluation

I learned something new.
Please explain your answer.

Strongly Agree	Agree	Disagree	Strongly Disagree

I am satisfied with my work.
Please explain your answer.

Strongly Agree	Agree	Disagree	Strongly Disagree

I showed concern for others.
Please explain your answer.

Strongly Agree	Agree	Disagree	Strongly Disagree

I was cooperative with my group members.
Please explain your answer.

Strongly Agree	Agree	Disagree	Strongly Disagree

I helped others in a meaningful way.
Please explain your answer.

Strongly Agree	Agree	Disagree	Strongly Disagree

My group members were cooperative.
Please explain your answer.

Strongly Agree	Agree	Disagree	Strongly Disagree

INDEX

ABOUT THE AUTHORS

Carrie Sorby Duits is the Lower School Division Head at Graland Country Day School in Denver, Colorado. She was an elementary school teacher for 16 years and has worked with teachers and preservice teachers as a clinical professor at the University of Colorado—Boulder.

As a curriculum developer, Ms. Duits co-authored NASA's *The Cassini Teacher Guide*, which focuses on the Cassini Mission to Saturn.

Adelle K. Dorman is a second/third grade teacher in Arlington, Virginia. She holds a Ph.D. in educational leadership and innovation from the University of Colorado—Boulder.

From *Teacher Ideas Press*

APPRECIATING DIVERSITY THROUGH CHILDREN'S LITERATURE:
Teaching Activities for the Primary Grades
Meredith McGowan, Patricia J. Wheeler, and Tom McGowan

Incorporating literature about diverse people into the curriculum encourages students to comprehend and value diversity. In this resource, stories that focus on four areas of diversity—age, gender, physical abilities, and ethnicity—provide the basis for activities that encourage children to think, empathize, and take action. **Grades 1–3.**
xvii, 135p. 8½x11 paper ISBN 1-56308-117-2

SOCIAL STUDIES THROUGH CHILDREN'S LITERATURE: An Integrated Approach
Anthony D. Fredericks

This activity-centered approach to elementary social studies features children's picture books that illustrate important social studies concepts. Fredericks shows you how to make connections between social studies and literature and how to use book webbing. **Grades K–5.**
xviii, 192p. 8½x11 paper ISBN 0-87287-970-4

GEOGRAPHIC LITERACY THROUGH CHILDREN'S LITERATURE
Linda K. Rogers

Combining practical, student-centered activities with an annotated bibliography of more than 160 children's books, this guide models ways for classroom teachers to teach geography through children's literature. **Grades K–6.**
ix, 161p. 8½x11 paper ISBN 1-56308-439-2

WRITING THROUGH CHILDREN'S AND YOUNG ADULT LITERATURE, GRADES 4–8:
From Authors to Authorship
Mary Strong and Mimi Neamen

This acclaimed book uses students' natural responses to literature to guide them into creative action. It teaches the writing process naturally, using published works as the basis for writing experiences. Literature-based writing ideas, examples of students' writing, and vignettes that describe students at work on different projects are included. **Grades 4–8.**
xi, 173p. 8½x11 paper ISBN 1-56308-038-9

INTERMEDIATE SCIENCE THROUGH CHILDREN'S LITERATURE: Over Land and Sea
Carol M. Butzow and John W. Butzow

These hands-on and discovery activities use scientific concepts and span all disciplines of the middle school curriculum. Focusing on earth and environmental science themes, topics such as oceans, rivers, mountains, air, weather, deserts, fossils, plant and environmental quality are covered. **Grades 4–7.**
xxv, 193p. 8½x11 paper ISBN 0-87287-946-1

MATH THROUGH CHILDREN'S LITERATURE: Making the NCTM Standards Come Alive
Kathryn L. Braddon, Nancy J. Hall, and Dale Taylor

Launch children into the world of mathematical literacy with books that give them the opportunity to experience the joy of math through their **own** understanding. Following the NCTM Standards, these literature activities are designed around an integrated reading process that captures a child's interest and brings math to life. **Grades 1–6.**
xviii, 218p. 8½x11 paper ISBN 0-87287-932-1

For a FREE catalog or to place an order, please contact:

Teacher Ideas Press
Dept. B64 · P.O. Box 6633 · Englewood, CO 80155-6633
1-800-237-6124, ext. 1 · Fax: 303-220-8843 · E-mail: lu-books@lu.com

Check out the TIP Web site!
www.lu.com/tip